How to handle the media

Politico's guide to

How to handle the media

Nicholas Comfort

Politico's
PUBLISHING

First published in Great Britain 2003
Politico's Publishing
8 Artillery Row
Westminster
London
SW1P 1RZ

www.politicos.co.uk/publishing

A catalogue record for this book is available from the British Library.

ISBN 1 84275 003 8

Printed and bound by Creative Print and Design

Contents

Preface   vii

1   How to get the media to work for you   1

2   Getting your story into print   43

3   Making an impact on television   67

4   Sounding your best on radio   97

5   Staging a successful press conference   115

6   Putting out an effective news release   138

7   Now it's up to you   158

Index   160

Preface

If you are having to deal for the first time with newspapers, radio and television, or already have such dealings and would welcome some practical tips, this book is for you. You may have a message to get across or an event to publicise, or you may have become, for reasons welcome or unwelcome, the focus of media attention. Either way, how you handle the media will determine what kind of impression you make on the public . . . if any. The techniques for making the most of the situation that I recommend in this book are tried and tested ones, and should help you cope in even the trickiest of circumstances. Some may appear blindingly obvious, but it's amazing how often people in such situations are tripped up by the simplest things: get them right, and you are well on the way to winning your argument.

Though I have worked in the media for over thirty years – mainly in newspapers but also in radio and public affairs – I am always myself a little hesitant when my counterparts want to interview or quote me for some reason. So I understand only too well the nervousness that most people outside the business feel when a newspaper reporter or television crew turns up on the doorstep, maybe to press them on a highly sensitive or personal matter. Yet I have also come to appreciate the professionalism with which most journalists operate, and their overriding interest in getting to the kernel of a story they think will interest the wider public . . . rather than in trying to harass, stitch up or humiliate their subjects. By the time you put this book down, you should feel more confident in dealing with them.

I have tried out and tested many of the techniques recommended here in media training sessions for Government press officers, UK business executives, and Ministers and human rights activists in Zambia. The techniques themselves are based primarily on my experiences as a working journalist, with the *Daily Telegraph*, the *Sun*, the *Guardian*, the *Independent on Sunday*, the *Sunday People*, *Scotland on Sunday*, the *European*, the *Daily Record*, the *Sheffield Morning Telegraph* and the *Northern Echo*. I have been fortunate to serve under some outstanding editors – I single out Bill Deedes, Max Hastings, Harold Evans and Endell Laird – and to work with, and compete against, true professionals who have freely shared their skills, their expertise and – when I was lucky – their stories. I have also been privileged to work with some of the BBC's finest radio producers.

Special thanks are due to my wife, Corinne Reed Comfort, not only for encouraging me in this project but for explaining to me the techniques she employed when Head of Communications for McDonald's UK, and before that for Shell. She has provided me with the insights and inspiration; any mistakes are my own.

Nicholas Comfort
Swalcliffe, Oxon.
November 2002

1 How to get the media to work for you

Your agenda – or theirs?

You have a story to tell, a cause to advocate, a business to promote – or maybe something to hide. In any of these circumstances, the agenda of the reporter who rings you up or knocks on your door may well be very different from yours. A journalist will, after all, be looking for the most marketable news story that can be crafted out of the facts available, and those facts may not always be convenient to you, nor the reporter's priorities necessarily the same as yours. Yet the moment that contact is established, you have access to the media, and the opportunity either to get over your story (or your side of it) to the public at large or to minimise the damage that a very difficult issue could cause you and those you care about. Whose agenda will make it into print or on to the broadcast news – theirs or yours? The choice is up to you.

The media have a job to do, an accepted role in our society and a clear idea of what makes a story. The old dictum that 'Dog bites man' isn't news, but 'Man bites dog' is a bankable story, still holds true. Yet with stories of quite startling degrees of weirdness from all over the world pouring into Britain's newsrooms 24 hours a day, it's easy for the issues that you or I wish to raise to end up on the spike. Which is why it is often better to target local newspapers, radio or television rather than try to obtain national coverage – unless your story is so unusual or genuinely important as to capture the interest of people all over the country. After all, only one or two stories a day make the front page of the *Sun*, and maybe six or eight on page one of the *Daily Telegraph*. That's how stiff the competition is.

Yet the criteria for what makes news are essentially the same – or should be – in the newsroom of the *Sun* and the office of the smallest local weekly. For a start, the information has to be fresh. There is no point in your bothering the media with something they already know about unless you can give them some worthwhile new angle to get them interested. It is also worth checking beforehand that they haven't published your story already. I once rang the *Times* diary to inform them that the president of one of the former Soviet republics had been stuck in the lift at the BBC, to be told: 'We carried it this morning. Didn't you read it?' An elementary check would have spared me embarrassment.

Yet just because something is new and verifiable, don't expect the person you call to shout 'Hold the front page!' – or to call a 'True story alert' as the legendary Kelvin McKenzie was wont to do at the *Sun* when one of his reporters argued that a story should be used because it was factual. For a news item also needs to be interesting to people other than yourself, and before you pick up the phone you should ask yourself whether anybody who doesn't know you would really be interested. A news item also needs to matter specifically to the people the news organisation is reporting to: a local community, an age group, an ethnic group or people with the same business interest or hobby. It has to be timely, too; there is no point in reporting a flower show held six months ago, or in trying to stir up interest in an event too far in advance. You need to catch the moment.

The more carefully you target your medium, the better the chance of getting your message or your story across. If you're staging a fishing competition, you don't contact a paper for pigeon fanciers. And if you're contacting local newspapers or radio stations, for heaven's sake make certain that they cover the location where the event is happening or the controversy has broken out. People in London trying to plant stories in the regions have a sorry track record of faxing the paper in Wakefield about something happening in Bradford and then being surprised that no one up there seems interested. So if you're operating outside an area or a speciality that you're familiar with, do your research.

Above all, the media are looking for something with an unusual twist – even 'Man bites dog' is pretty tame compared with 'Freddie Starr ate my hamster'. So the less routine and humdrum the message you want to put across, the better your chance of the newspaper, television or radio station you have targeted allocating precious space to report it.

The smarter you are in selling your story, the more likely you are to force it on to the radar screens of the men and women who decide what the public actually gets to read and hear about. Conversely, if you botch your approach to the media they may well think twice about calling you if the issue comes up again. But with a little thought and preparation, you can succeed in finding a niche for even the most basic item of news; after all, many local free newspapers are delighted to carry reports of everyday community events provided someone else does the work of putting the story together.

Conversely, if a newspaper or radio station has the bit between its teeth about some event or issue that you find inconvenient and embarrassing, you can't simply ring down the shutters and say 'No comment.' That will merely ensure bad publicity and an assumption of guilt on your part by anyone who reads or hears the story. Instead, you should try to turn the situation to your advantage even if you can't, there is still scope for you to limit the damage.

Always remember: most of the men and women in public life whose careers are ruined by exposure in the media are not particularly liked by their colleagues, have enemies who have been waiting for an opportunity to strike, or have not impressed those journalists who deal with them regularly. When they hit choppy water, they go under. Those who survive, or live to fight another day after their seamy side has been revealed in the tabloids, are people either who are rated basically decent by those who know them, or who have cultivated the media when it mattered.

The former Conservative Party chairman Cecil Parkinson, at the height of the scandal over his love child by the Commons secretary Sara Keays, bought himself incalculable media goodwill by letting the press pack outside his house camp out in his garage and bringing them a bottle of whisky. He was still forced to resign a few days later as Trade and Industry Secretary following further revelations, but he was soon rehabilitated – with the media at least – and was able to make a Cabinet comeback. A display of kindness and basic decency – though not, I should stress, bribery, which will merely make your reputation worse – can make an impression in even the most unpleasant situation.

If things get really grim for you and your family, you may well be tempted to take a sudden sunshine break or go to ground in some friend's ancestral pile. If you are lucky, you may be able to evade the media in this way until interest in the story you are at the centre of has died down. But there are several powerful caveats.

First of all, the press are very good at finding people who don't want to be found, and it will generally look worse for you if you face them after having run away rather than when the story breaks – it makes you look as if you have been cornered. You can get away with taking a few days to compose your thoughts and then inviting the media to meet you – but if they get to you first, you will have lost the high ground.

Second, don't expect all your friends to be as loyal as you would wish; one of them may very well tip off the press as to where you have gone, and not necessarily for money.

Third, you can actually gain Brownie points with the media – and more favourable coverage – by facing the music. Jeffrey Archer's stock, with me at least, rose considerably when after resigning as deputy chairman of the Conservative Party in 1986 he didn't make a dash for it, but stayed home and answered the phone himself. His rehabilitation would turn out not to be permanent, but for me he got it off to a very good start.

Before you make contact

If you have a story to put across – and all the more so if it could be an awkward one for you – you need to sit down at an early stage and work out a strategy for releasing it to the media. If they are going to find out anyway, it's best that they hear it from you. This way, you have some chance of determining how your difficulties are reported, rather than leaving the initiative to some individual or group with an axe to grind. If more than one news organisation is likely to be interested, it's important that they all hear about it at the same time – if you give a major story first to one favoured reporter, the others will dislike you for it and their coverage may be slanted against you.

You need first to work out the best time from your point of view for breaking the story: not so early that the opposition has a chance to build, nor so late that you can be accused of 'bouncing' your critics. If you want to make an impact, embargoing your story for use on a Monday morning or the day after a Bank Holiday will give you a flying start as there will be little other news around. But you can never guarantee that other stories won't get in the way: a colleague of mine once rushed breathless into the office and told his night editor: 'I've got the front page – they've just sacked the Chief

Constable!' only to be told: 'No you haven't – Kennedy's been shot.' My own first real exclusive ended up way down the page because it coincided with Neil Armstrong landing on the moon. Sometimes news won't keep.

No matter how simple your message or how confident you are of your ability to put it across, it's unwise just to pick up the phone to the media and spout – not least because if you cold-call a radio station they might put you straight on the air. There's nothing worse for a reporter under pressure than getting a call from someone who hasn't prepared or doesn't seem to know what they are trying to say. The better briefed and organised you are and the better equipped to answer a reporter's questions, the more conviction you will carry and the greater your chance of securing the air time or column inches you want.

The first question you need to ask yourself is: 'What am I trying to achieve?' Who are you trying to reach? What message do you want to leave readers or listeners with, assuming the story does get reported? And what can you say to the reporter which will make that message seem important? You need to marshal the basic facts that make the story interesting and relevant, singling out points that are topical, unusual or of human or local interest. It makes sense to jot them down and use them as an aide-memoire when you and the reporter are talking; there's nothing worse than hanging up and realising you've forgotten to mention some basic fact.

You also need to ask yourself whether going public is wise. All of us know things the papers would love to print . . . but it's easy to pick your paper off the doormat the morning after you have told all and realise, when you see how the story has been treated and how it will look to everybody else, that disclosure was not the most sensible course for you. And that applies even more to disclosures you make about other people.

If there could be two sides to the issue, you should rehearse your arguments and anticipate questions an interested journalist might ask. It's well worth taking time, too, to identify and rule out points you don't really need to make, so as to keep the issue simple. The biggest turn-off for anyone in journalism is the enthusiast who rambles on for ever without getting to the point, or presents a story of such complexity as to baffle the most patient and insightful reporter.

If you are representing an organisation, be it humble or prestigious, it's also important to work out who would put your case to greatest effect. You need to field someone who can explain the story so that it is readily understood, someone who can be personable and persuasive but not overbearing. This is particularly important if a broadcast interview is in prospect: some people sound a lot better than they look, so are better not doing television, and some very photogenic people have voices that are too thin for radio. (It may sound chauvinistic, but for this reason men generally come over better on radio than women.) And once your group has decided who to put before the mike or the camera, it's worth having a quick rehearsal so that they get used to tackling the most obvious questions they will face – and to lessen the chances of their turning into a loose cannon on the air.

If a group of you are seeking publicity, it may be possible to divide up the interviews without causing offence, so that no bids have to be turned down and everyone plays to their strengths – in my experience, only about one person in thirty needs to be actively kept away from the camera or the mike because of their inability to express themselves. Equally, you don't have to look like a film star to come over well on television, though it is a fact of life that a pretty girl is more likely get her picture in the paper (and maybe get your story across at the same time) than Mr Average. So are children and animals, if relevant in any way to your story.

Just one note of caution – a long, shot, this but an important check to make. You need to make sure that if you or any of your colleagues are going to receive heavy media exposure, nothing is going to leap out of your or their past – or their present, for that matter – that would detract from the message you want to put across. There's more than one instance of someone going to the Sunday papers with story A and finding themselves the star of unflattering story B that had been lurking in the undergrowth. Particularly if you are dealing with the tabloids, it's worth just mentioning this risk – without, of course, pointing the finger of suspicion at anyone. And don't forget to put yourself through the same process. The last thing your campaign could do with is a headline like 'Man fined last year for not paying his fare heads crusade for more buses'. It does happen.

If you find yourself attracting a lot of media interest or want to generate publicity over a period, it's worth compiling a 'grid': make a note of all the news organisations who are interested or whom you want to engage, work out when it would suit you to receive publicity from them and when interviews etc. would have to take place, and record contact numbers for the journalists involved. Your grid will keep changing and much of the activity listed on it won't happen when you expect it to, but you will have kept some control of the agenda. And one word of warning never give out any information to the media before you are ready for it to appear. A reporter may tell you his article is planned in for a fortnight's time, but his editor may decide it's too good to keep.

In going to the media to announce a decision or give your side of a story you can either put out (by post, e-mail or fax) a press release (see Chapter 6), stating the basic facts of the situation but with your own interpretative gloss, or if the issue is really sensitive or complex you can invite the media to send reporters to a briefing or press conference (see Chapter 5) at which you can hand out the release and explain it. This way you have the best chance of gaining some control over the situation – provided you make a conscious effort to keep in touch with the reporters who have attended the briefing if it is a story on which the comments of other people will be sought.

If your announcement has strong visual potential, it's worth staging a photocall, inviting news photographers through their papers' picture desks as well as television crews. Reporters may also attend to provide the words to match, but a strong picture will make your point.

Incidentally, it is best to invite reporters personally to a briefing to increase the chances of their turning up – and follow up with a phone call to gauge their interest and availability and give them any extra information they may need in advance. News organisations appreciate this, because if the reporter you have targeted isn't free they have the chance to send someone else.

Do I need help?

Having worked out what you want to say and how you want to say it, which news organisation(s) would you do best to call? Is this a story that would genuinely interest the national press or television, or is it of basically local or regional concern? Might some specialist publication for, say, environmentalists, car enthusiasts or computer users be interested? Would the story, or someone involved in it, make a good picture or an interesting subject for television, or would it play better on radio? Think of the possibilities: don't just contact the paper you usually read or the radio station you listen to, but consider it a question of horses for courses. Who would be most likely to report what you have to say, and report it in a way that will do your cause the most good? And if a newspaper, does it come out on the day of the week that would be of most use for you?

The merits of newspapers, television and radio for getting your case across are summed up later on. But there are alternatives to contacting any of the media direct, and the most obvious is to contact a public relations firm. If your business is planning a long-running campaign to attract public or consumer interest, or if you are a reasonably well-heeled pressure group, it is well worth contacting a PR professional and discussing your needs with them; you will find them in every reasonable-sized town, and they don't all charge London prices. But you need to shop around: some public relations firms specialise in crisis management, organising events or promoting issues; others are great at getting journalists to consume alcohol at your expense or at introducing their clients to each other, but are of no practical use in getting a story across. Above all, most (though astonishingly not all) PR firms are dab hands at promoting themselves – it is only worth your while taking one on if they can perform the same service for you. And if you haven't much cash and can find the time to run your own campaign or handle your own issue, you are best advised to go for it yourself.

Instead of approaching a PR firm, you can – particularly if you have a one-off story to market – go through a news agency. There are such agencies – or at any rate freelance journalists selling stories to the medium most likely to be interested – all over the country, and on routine stories the national media often ask a local agency to do the footwork for them. Indeed, if someone rings representing, say, the *Daily Mail*, it's always worth asking if they are a staff reporter or working for a local agency. If the latter, you should ask whether the paper has commissioned the story or is taking it from the journalist on spec.

A local freelance will usually expect you to deal with them exclusively; a friend or neighbour may even know such a journalist and suggest that you contact them yourself. In my experience, local agency reporters are just as ethical and conscientious as those on the staff of newspapers or broadcasting organisations, and unlike a PR firm they won't charge you – it would be a severe breach of ethics for any journalist to do so. Freelances have the advantage of already having a foot in the door when it comes to interesting a news organisation in your story. But there is also one major disadvantage: the moment you let them act on your behalf, you lose control. News desks contacted will see your issue through the eyes of the freelance getting in touch, not through yours. And that can be critical.

Still, if you're a busy person and simply don't have the time to contact the media yourself, this is one avenue to consider. Indeed, I knew one Member of Parliament who simply handed all his constituency correspondence over to the local freelance, to turn anything he could into a news story. In doing so, however, he upset every other local reporter and news organisation, as they all had to pay the freelance for information a more assiduous MP would have passed free of charge to local papers, radio and television. So don't go down that particular route if you want to keep the local media on your side.

If you have a really sensational story to tell or are in serious personal trouble, it's tempting to go for the nuclear option and call in one of the celebrity PR handlers – the name of Max Clifford comes most readily to mind, but there are others. They don't come cheap, so unless you expect to be paid handsomely for your story or are playing for very high stakes, this isn't a course to consider. The plus is that the person you go to will be on first-name terms with most tabloid editors and key figures in broadcasting and may be able to negotiate a very good deal for you; the downside, as ever, is that you risk losing control of the story. Just before she was killed in a plane crash, the American singer Aaliyah came to London to give interviews, accompanied by a PR handler who warned reporters not to question her about a particular past relationship. Up to that moment, they had known nothing about it, so that story inevitably and counterproductively became the subject of the interviews.

Nevertheless, if you have a sensational story to market, the Max Cliffords of this world can handle the media for you, and if you are in a really tight corner, they may well be able to help you come up smelling of something like roses.

But whether you call in an expert to help or not, *never* say more than you think is sensible or you may end up with a PR disaster. Remember the late lamented Tory MP Geoffrey Dickens? He called a press conference on the serious subject of paedophilia, at which he ensured himself zero coverage of the issue by also announcing that he was leaving his wife for a nurse he had met (though he later went back to his wife). He equally foolishly asked reporters not to ring Mrs Dickens until he had broken the news to her. You can imagine the headlines the next day.

Whom should I call?

Having selected your news medium, you next need to decide who to contact within that organisation. If your story concerns your local council and you know the name of the journalist who usually reports its proceedings, try to speak to him or her. If you are offering fresh information on a story written by a particular reporter, contact them direct. But if you have a news item of general interest, don't cold-call a journalist simply because you've seen their name in print or heard them on the air; quite apart from anything else, it may be their day off. Equally, unless you live in a small community where the newspaper office or radio station is open to all, don't just walk in: most news editors assume – wrongly, in my experience – that anyone who comes in off the street is a crank, or worse still someone with a hugely complicated story that will take days of staff time to get to the bottom of and probably isn't worth the trouble.

You can find any news organisation in the phone book, and their switchboard will put you through to the person you want to speak to. For media out of your area, check the reference section of your local library if you have time – or if you know the name of the newspaper or radio station just call Directory Enquiries to find the number.

The most effective way of placing your story is to call the news desk of the media organisation you have decided on, say who you are and what organisation (if any) you represent, lay out in a couple of phrases the barest bones of the story and ask who you can speak to. But unless the person on the news desk specifically asks you to tell them more (in a really small outfit the news team may consist of just one person), don't cut loose and deluge them with information: just say enough to get them interested. Then, when you get through to the reporter, say once again who you are and talk them through your story, keeping one eye on your crib sheet.

If your story concerns your business, it's best – unless the tale is one of human interest – to ask to speak to the business editor of the media organisation you have targeted; most now have such a person co-ordinating business coverage, though astonishingly the BBC only recently appointed its first business editor. And equally, if your story would work best on the sports pages, ring the sports desk.

If the issue you want to highlight is not immediate, hard news but still of public interest – for example, if you are starting a campaign on a health, education or other social issue – you should ask to speak in the first instance to the features editor. The features pages in the middle of newspapers both national and local, and magazine programmes on the radio, have far more space and time than the news pages or bulletins to deal with a subject in detail, and if you have a story of human interest to tell they may well be your best port of call unless the issue is pressing. Just one warning. Newspaper features departments lack the sense of urgency, and often the organisation, of news desks. Things have a nasty habit of getting lost or forgotten, e-mails don't always get read and you may have to make follow-up calls to make certain that anything happens.

Newspaper feature pages overlap the role of magazines, and it may be worth trying for coverage in the latter as long as you realise that magazines do their planning weeks or even months ahead. The most sensible thing to do before contacting a magazine is to buy a copy and look through the list of staff at the front to see who the best person to call might be. You will also get a feel from reading the magazine as to whether the kind of article you have in mind is indeed something they might be interested in. Check in particular that they have space for feature articles on subjects of general interest: if not, cut your losses and try elsewhere.

If they approach you

Of course, the media may contact you rather than the other way round. You shouldn't assume if a journalist calls you that something has gone horribly wrong or that you are in the dock; he or she may simply be trying to establish some simple fact or be interested in a matter you will be happy to discuss. But equally you want to be careful what you say, and above all what you are quoted as saying. I recall the member of a residents' group complaining about the odour from a sewage works telling the *Sheffield Star*: 'We had relations last week and the smell was terrible.' You can guess what she meant, but we are all left with a very different – and rather more intriguing – image.

So you need to ask yourself as quickly as possible after you pick up the phone: 'Why do they want to speak to me?'; 'Is it in my interest to talk to them at all?' and if so, 'Would it be best if I asked them to call back once I've got my facts in order?'

Unless they are up against a deadline, no self-respecting journalist will mind if you ask for a few minutes to marshal the facts. After all, they may have been working on the story for days and it may be something you have long forgotten about. Equally, you are quite within your rights when they ring back to say that, having thought about it, you don't think there is much you can usefully contribute. The advantage of buying a little time is that if you are not used to dealing with the media as a matter of course, then get a phone call out of the blue and start talking, it's easy to say more than you mean to – and then very hard to row back.

Even if the journalist insists he or she is doing you a favour by inviting you to put your side of the story, make quite sure that you do want to get involved. Unless the story revolves directly around you – a situation where a journalist will persevere even with a reluctant interviewee – your caller will only be trying to coax a few facts out of you. If you are not forthcoming, he or she will eventually give up – all the quicker if you can suggest that someone else knows more than you do or may be readier to talk. And if you really don't want to see your name in the papers or on television but have information relevant to the story which you are happy to see in print, maybe to correct a false impression, you can always ask to be treated as a 'source'. This isn't the same as saying 'No comment'; it's a way of helping the reporter establish the truth. Unless it would make nonsense of the story not to mention your name, a good reporter will normally agree.

If the questioning is head-on, like 'Have you left your family to set up home with the church organist?', your choices are more limited, unless the story is false, in which case you can simply deny it. Your word alone may not suffice; the journalist will probably want also to speak to your life partner, who in such circumstances will be even angrier about the untruth than you are.

But you don't have to decide instantaneously whether to come clean or tell the reporter you have nothing to say. You can first try to ascertain how much the reporter actually knows. He or she may only have the wildest of rumours to go on, in which case you can sidetrack them. Or they may already have corroboration from everyone else involved in the story, in which case a few dignified words of agreement will serve you far better than a blustery denial which will make you look even worse when the story appears. If the reporter presses you on some sensitive issue that has yet to come to a head, you are perfectly within your rights to make a 'holding comment' – for instance, that things are at a very delicate stage and it would be wrong/unfair to say anything at present, but that you will talk more freely once you are able to.

Of course, the journalist may just turn up on your doorstep. Now that most people have a phone, this tends to happen only if the reporter suspects you will otherwise be reluctant to talk, if the media are looking for reactions to some event in your immediate neighbourhood, or if they need a photo of someone who has become news – most often, though not always, sad news.

In my experience, even people who have been through a terrible personal tragedy may be ready or even eager to talk to a visiting reporter. I shall never forget the mother of a five-year-old boy on Teesside who had just been run over and killed while playing outside his front gate inviting me in and handing me his picture, 'so that everyone else can see what a lovely boy I had until he was taken from me'. I felt like an intruder as I knocked on the door, and not much better when I left, despite her sitting me down with a cup of tea and showing me the family photo album, but for her my visit was part of the grieving process. The little boy's picture in the next day's *Northern Echo* was the best tribute she could pay him.

If a reporter calls at a moment of private grief and you ask them politely to leave, they will almost invariably do so; if they won't, call their editor, and if that doesn't work call the police. But such situations can be an ordeal for the journalist too: the worst nightmare for any reporter is to knock on the door of someone who has just been bereaved and discover that no one has told them yet. Several colleagues have suffered this ultimate embarrassment.

For most members of the public, thankfully, this kind of scenario will never arise. And if a reporter calls about some issue where you do know the facts and want the public to know them, you should give your full co-operation; it will be genuinely appreciated, and could be the basis of a relationship that will be beneficial to you both. When I worked on a local newspaper, I built up a valuable bank of contacts: ordinary people I came across while working on one story who could help me later with others, or who simply became friends. And you don't get friendship without trust.

What are journalists like?

The one attribute all journalists need to have is a thirst, and a nose, for news. A few plodders do get into the business, but the number who watch the clock religiously or who go to report a wedding, find that the bride or groom hasn't turned up and go back to the office saying that nothing happened is fortunately few. A few do impose absurd demarcation lines, like the sports writer on one national paper who refused to report a racist attack from the crowd on a black Test cricketer because it wasn't part of the game; understandably, he didn't last long. But almost every reporter has an imagination for you to capture, and a sense of fairness to appeal to. It's up to you to create and then to seize your opportunity.

Dismiss from your mind all those stereotypes from the black-and-white movies: no one in a British newsroom in living memory has worn an eyeshade, unless suffering from some rare optical condition, and not all journalists are scruffy, booze-wracked men in late middle age. Sex equality came early to Fleet Street and to broadcasting, and you are just as likely to be interviewed by a woman. And *never* make the mistake of imagining that a woman journalist will only be writing for the women's page!

The journalist you encounter is increasingly likely to come from an ethnic minority, with broadcasting attracting more ethnic recruits than the written media. He or she is also far more likely than twenty years ago to have a university degree – though not necessarily in journalism and certainly not in media studies, a discipline scorned as a pseudo-academic irrelevance by most working journalists and news executives. Until quite recently, most journalists learned their craft in the 'university of life' after leaving school at sixteen or eighteen. When I joined the *Daily Telegraph*'s Parliamentary and political reporting team in 1978, I was the only one out of eight top-flight journalists there to have a degree. It's very different now. Local newspaper proprietors have traditionally preferred to hire school leavers, given the chance, because they could be paid less, would be easier to train and would ask fewer questions. But many of these have gone right to the top.

A reporter working for your local paper or radio station will not necessarily be familiar with the area; they may well have come recently from another part of the country and need to have community issues and even local geography explained to them. If you have the slightest hint of this when you are being interviewed, you should check to make sure your journalist knows the correct spelling of place and street names; nothing looks worse in a local paper than a misspelt or misheard name that is familiar to every reader: it destroys the authority of the article.

The reporter you meet will probably be under forty, and may be half that age. Yet even though journalism is now, more than ever, a business for the young, most national newspapers and the more sensible regional media still have a nucleus of older staffers who have seen it all and can assess the most complex situation quickly, condensing its essence into just a few paragraphs. Older reporters are highly adept at wheedling information out of reluctant sources, but they are also masters of detail and, most important – for you as well as for them – they get it right. For one thing, they will usually have an impeccable shorthand note of your conversation rather than having to rely on a tape recorder that is prone to malfunction, as mine once did when I was interviewing Tony Blair. But whatever a journalist's age, origins or educational background, he or she will almost certainly have a quick mind and an ability to grasp the essentials of a story. It is up to you to make sure your message or version of events is put over so that it gets grasped.

Journalists come in all shapes and sizes, and vary in appearance from the stylish to the slovenly. Don't be lulled into a false sense of security if someone unkempt turns up to interview you; they may still have the sharpest of minds. And whatever you do, you should never underestimate their intelligence or their ability to communicate any misgivings they may have about you to others.

Most reporters are personable or at least polite, though a few lack social graces and can irritate any interviewee. Like the rest of us, they can be unfocused, irritating, ignorant, tricky or even rude, or simply have a bad day. On the rare occasions you do encounter boorish behaviour from a reporter, you should try to rise above it to make sure your case gets across. But if he or she is downright objectionable, you should certainly complain to their editor – and if you are harassed, you have the right to go to the Press Complaints Commission if the paper in question offers no redress.

Except on the rare occasions when things do turn nasty, you should never take probing or even hostile questions personally; the journalist isn't trying to insult you by pressing you hard, but simply trying to ascertain the facts or get you to argue your case so as to bring out the most powerful quotes. And if you lose your cool, they may conclude, quite reasonably, that you have something to hide or are up to no good.

Equally, you should never assume that just because a paper or programme seems biased against you or what you are doing, a reporter from it will share those prejudices. Even those news organ-isations with a strong political slant generally hire their staff on grounds of ability rather than because of their opinions – big-name columnists excepted. You cannot guarantee that what you tell a reporter from such a medium will make it into print or on to the air – but if you don't tell them, it certainly won't. So take just as much time and trouble as you would with a 'friendly' paper, more indeed, as you may need to explain your thinking in greater detail. But do take extra care not to say anything that could be twisted into use against you – no matter how friendly the reporter may seem, they may just be tempting you to lower your guard. In just the same way, be careful of what you say to a reporter in a casual conversation, and if you think you have just been a little too candid, tell them politely but firmly: 'That is not for use.'

Where should we meet?

If a journalist does call you, they may simply need a few simple facts which can be tied up in a brief conversation on the phone. But if they want to know more, they may suggest meeting you or your colleagues in the organisation you represent, and that raises a further question: where should you meet them? Where the story concerns you as an individual or as a member of your community, it's natural for them to come to your home; they want the story so they will expect to travel. If they do, you should arrange the meeting at a time that fits in with your domestic routine and leaves you enough time not just to marshal what you want to say or prepare for difficult questions, but to search out any paperwork or pictures that may be useful to you in presenting your arguments or, if you are seeking publicity, to help the reporter in crafting the story. You may be able to nudge the story into print on your terms by preparing a press release (see Chapter 6) or even, if you think the issue important enough, staging a press conference (see Chapter 5).

If the story concerns your business and the media have contacted you, it would make sense for the reporter to come to your office to interview you. But if they are likely to be confronted outside your premises by demonstrators or strikers who can get their side of the story in first or make an embarrassing picture or a scene for the television cameras, you should arrange to meet them somewhere else.

If you are seeking publicity for an organisation – say a charity – that has an office or other premises, it may make sense to meet the reporter there rather than at your home, so that they can meet your colleagues or check anything you want to show them from your files. If that organisation does something with people – a day nursery, a youth or old folk's club, an environmental clean-up or protest group – it's well worth suggesting that you meet the reporter where and when the activity takes place, and that he or she bring a photographer or cameraman with them.

If you are meeting the media in a location where space is at a premium – on a crowded factory floor or inside a tiny building, for example – and interest in the story is intense, you are quite within your rights to organise a 'pool' of reporters to prevent the media presence getting out of hand. Buckingham Palace does this all the time, so that when the Queen visits someone in their home they are not overwhelmed by reporters and cameras. You normally pick a handful of reporters – say the Press Association, one television, one radio, one national press, one local, plus a stills photographer – who attend the event on the strict understanding that they will make the information they garner available to all other journalists who are covering the story. This isn't news management – it's common sense, and while reporters may argue about who is in the pool, they won't dispute the principle.

The reason for this is that an excessive media scrum gets in the way of the story, causes bad blood between news organisations and can be a threat to public safety. Most reporters and photographers have seen too many free-for-alls where nobody came out with the story. I remember the media stampede at Harry Ramsden's original chip shop at Guiseley when Margaret Thatcher descended on it in mid-campaign – and a distinguished television anchorman ripping local Tories' election placards out of the way to give his crew a clear shot. Television crews and photographers are at their worst in such situations for entirely understandable reasons – they have to get the picture, and if anything or anybody gets in the way they might as well not have been there.

Occasionally it may suit you (or the reporter) if you drop by their office to be interviewed, but there are two drawbacks to this where newspapers are concerned. First: you are on their turf instead of your own and it's harder to keep control of the interview. And second: most newspapers don't have anywhere quiet enough on the premises to hold a private and sensible conversation. By contrast, most radio stations will prefer to interview you in their own studio rather than over the phone; the sound quality is better and an interview is livelier if the participants are face to face. You should be ready to go along with this unless it is highly inconvenient. And if you have any distance to travel and the radio station has invited you, make sure it pays for a taxi.

Taking and keeping control

No matter who is to blame for a difficult situation, it is vital that when you are in contact with the media you take and keep control – not in an aggressive sense but by making sure that the argument, and hopefully the resulting story, is very much on your terms. Some of the techniques I have already discussed will serve you in good stead: jotting down vital points you want to get across, eliminating those that don't matter and will get in the way, rehearsing an interview beforehand. But you can do much more than that to control the story without in any way overstepping the mark.

Almost every decision any individual or organisation takes will affect other people. If they are affected for the worse, they will not like it. And if the issue is important for them and they haven't been properly consulted, they may very well take their complaint to the media – maybe using the techniques outlined in this book to give their complaint the greatest impact. But the people who take those decisions should also realise the importance of getting it right in the first place, or at the very least realise that what they are doing may prove unpopular and that they may need to take steps to get the media on their side before it turns hostile. Planning for such a situation can never start too soon.

In an ideal world, people and organisations taking any decision would ask themselves whether it could lead to a public relations disaster – or at the very least whether it will affect the public and they should be told about it. Yet you only have to switch on the news or pick up a paper to realise that politicians, business executives and others in authority are highly capable of misunderstanding or ignoring the public mood. I remember only too clearly the day a new authority took control of Sheffield's bus services and changed several route numbers without bothering to inform the public. Calls flooded in to the local paper from baffled commuters whose usual bus hadn't turned up, and when I rang the man in charge he told me: 'We didn't think the public would need to know.'

So if you are a bank planning to close rural branches, a football club proposing to sell its star player or a local council reducing library opening hours, you should be asking at the very outset: 'Should the public be told about this?', 'How will it look?' and 'If it looks bad, do we really have to do it?' The decision may still have to be taken, but at least you know you will have to work at selling it. And the same applies if you're a householder about to plant a row of leylandii and wipe out your neighbour's view, or planning to take up a really antisocial hobby. If you do go ahead regardless of the possible fallout, you will need to put over the best possible case when, eventually, the people affected by your decision contact the media.

If you come under fire in or from the media, you will do yourself no favours if you go to ground or try to play hide-and-seek; all that will do is confirm the impression, correct or otherwise, that you are culpable. Nothing looks worse on the evening news than someone in the headlines shielding their face with a newspaper as they leave work, or refusing to comment as they put their car in the garage and slam their front door behind them. Except, that is, if they assault the journalist who is trying to interview them, something even High Court judges have done from time to time and which makes great – and very damaging – television. The Lord Chancellor has now sent out advice to all judges on how to deal with 'doorstepping', reminding them that reporters are only doing their job and urging them to avoid displays of arrogance but say politely: 'I'm sorry, but I am unable to discuss this matter outside the court.'

Not all the individuals who leave court with a blanket over their heads have chosen this course of action, by the way. Sometimes it is essential for the fair conduct of a criminal case that pictures of the accused do not appear in the press or on television. (But if the police or your lawyer suggest that you do this, you will know you are in very deep trouble.)

A person involved in a highly controversial story who has been 'bought up' by one of the tabloids will be shielded from photographers working for rival media. The ultimate episode of this kind occurred in Glasgow when a man due in court charged with being drunk in charge of his dog was bought up by a newspaper whose photographer used the 'paper bag over the head' technique outside the building to deny a rival paper a clear shot. Perspicaciously, he put the bag over the dog's head, not that of the accused – he knew what would make the better picture.

There may not seem much to be gained by brazening it out and letting the cameras catch you at one of the low points in your life. But the media don't give up easily, so if they turn up and you realise you will have to make some comment sooner or later, it makes sense to let them know you are prepared to see them. Consult your family, your colleagues or your solicitor about what you are going to say, then go down and say it in as dignified a way as you can manage. And I repeat, never say: 'No comment.'

If you show that you have the guts and the decency to face your accusers, some at least of the people watching will be ready to listen to what you have to say. That's the first step towards taking control. And provided you can put across a serious argument or explanation and don't appear disdainful or overconfident, you may well find your side of the story taking hold. Just look at the way the former Railtrack chief executive Gerald Corbett won considerable public respect for himself, and a breathing space for his embattled company, by facing the cameras with candour in the weeks after the Ladbroke Grove and Hatfield disasters.

If things are not that fraught but you are still daunted by the prospect of reporters questioning you, there are other steps open to you to take control of an interview, or at least make sure the argument doesn't slip away from you. For a start, you need to match the mood of the occasion; if it's serious, wear sober clothing and don't show any signs of levity. This applies as much in dealing with the written press as with the cameras. Inappropriate clothing, gestures and comments come across terribly and not only on television: any newspaper journalist worth his or her salt can slip into their story a few phrases about your demeanour that will seriously undermine your credibility.

You also have the opportunity to influence how the story looks or sounds through your choice of words. You never want to make light of a difficult situation if that is what you are being questioned about, but it is all too easy to put an unnecessarily negative spin on it by the repeated use of words like 'problem', 'difficulty', 'unable', 'lost', 'defeat', 'struggle' or 'disaster'. Use 'challenge' instead of 'problem', 'crusade' instead of 'struggle', and you are off the back foot and starting to score a few runs.

You should equally be wary of using, particularly in broadcast interviews, combinations of words that send out a negative or unfortunate impression. 'Happy' combined with 'pain' suggests either masochism or heartlessness. My own favourite pairing to be avoided was used in an interview by an explosives factory manager whom I media-trained: you can imagine what effect juxtaposing the words 'explosion' and 'normal' would have had on residents concerned about safety at the plant.

Just as important, you shouldn't let the interviewer – even if it's Jeremy Paxman – get away unchallenged with a negative line of questioning. This is most important with television and radio interviews, where the audience will actually hear those questions. But even if you have a newspaper reporter conducting an interview in your sitting room, it's vital for you to make sure they get their facts straight, that you display confidence in your situation unless it is completely untenable, and even then come out with your self-respect intact. If there's nothing factually wrong with the questions the reporter is asking but they still sound horribly negative when strung together, tell him or her just that and then briefly restate your position in positive terms.

One thing you should always remember is that once you have opened up a subject, the journalists will know there is an issue to be probed – you can't shut it down again. So if you don't feel happy with a particular aspect of the matter in hand – say, that you are having problems with the planning authority – don't even hint at it. Once it's out, it's out.

If you have the slightest concern about how you will come out of the interview, you would be wise to tape it. The reporter will be keeping a full record of what is said, and you are fully entitled to do the same. Moreover, the very fact that you have your own tape running will deter the less scrupulous journalist from taking liberties with what you say. Tony Benn has done it for forty years.

When the interview comes to an end, there is more you can do to maintain control, or at least increase the chances of getting your point across. For a start, if you don't know a fact but can find it out, you might offer to check it or look it up and call the reporter with the information. But if you promise to ring back, make sure you do it in reasonably good time or you will forfeit much of the goodwill you have built up. Ringing back also gives you an opportunity to speak to the reporter as the story is being drafted; you can ask them if there is anything else they need, and gain some sense of whether you have got your point across. If you suspect you haven't, make that point again – but briefly. It's tempting to ask the journalist if you can see what they have written about you before it appears. Naturally, you want to make sure they have got their facts right. But most newspapers have a firm policy of not allowing this – to them it smacks of censorship. So it's better not to ask.

Be selective about how much you try to feed in after the interview. Reporters, particularly those on deadlines, don't like being barraged with supplementary material once they've started putting their story together – particularly if what they are told adds nothing. But they do appreciate being told of any last-minute developments; there is nothing worse for a journalist than knowing that what they have written or broadcast had already been overtaken by events, and that someone could have told them.

As I mentioned earlier, your contact with a journalist could very well be the start of a useful relationship, and this works both ways. If you are involved in an ongoing project or campaign or are likely to need media coverage for something else, it is in your interests to build a range of regular contacts – and if several journalists have been in touch, you have a useful base to build on.

If you can sense that the story will put you in the dock, you have a nervous few hours or days ahead of you until it appears. The knowledge that one of the Sunday tabloids is going to destroy your credibility creates a unique sense of despair. But don't panic. Don't tell your friends – unless they're affected by the story. And don't ring the paper and beg them not to print it – your call might have the opposite effect. If you're worried how the story will turn out, use the time before it appears (if it actually does) to rehearse what you will say to other journalists who follow it up. That will be time well spent.

If you feel the story has turned out well, you can always call the journalist who wrote or broadcast it, compliment them and offer them material for a follow-up piece. If there is no obvious sequel, just say you'll be happy to help if anything comes up in the future. You can then keep in touch, but you mustn't overdo it by badgering them with trivia; every reporter has at least one helpful informant whom they end up trying to avoid.

As you build a working relationship with a journalist, you can ask for advice on how you can develop your story or campaign in ways that would be of most use to the media as well as to yourself, or indeed on how other potential news items would play. Nine times out of ten, you will get sensible and objective advice, and the journalist won't mind if you take the next story to another medium if theirs wouldn't be able to do it justice. If you have the chance to keep up with several journalists on varying types of media, take it – you never know which of them will come in most useful next time. And if you're dealing with something of obvious interest to the national media, try not to deal always with one favourite reporter – the others won't like it and will take less interest in the story. Learn from the way the media turned against Princess Diana's butler Paul Burrell after his exclusive and lucrative deal with the Daily Mirror – he could have spread his revelations around and emerged unscathed.

Rebuttal

A recently developed and highly specialised technique is that of rebuttal: strong and speedy action to deny, correct, dispute or discredit a high-profile and damaging story about your party, company or organisation when it is broken by the media. Starting maybe with a single television or newspaper report, you will suddenly find yourself or your colleagues accused of conniving at some practice that puts the environment in peril, planning some course of action that will ruin the lives of a community or a workforce, or preparing to embark on some other highly controversial and potentially damaging policy. Sometimes the story will be downright wrong, sometimes it will be partly true, and on other occasions it will be alarmingly accurate; yet in every case it will be at best highly embarrassing and at worst commercially or politically disastrous. And as James Callaghan famously remarked (quoting the Victorian evangelist Dr Spurgeon), a lie can be halfway round the world before the truth has got its boots on.

It was to counter such reporting, and undo as much of the damage as possible, that the art of rebuttal was devised, surfacing first of all in the Labour Party's campaigning prior to its 1997 election victory. There are two aspects to rebuttal: knowing enough about what your own organisation is up to so that you are ready for hostile reporting of most of its activities, and having ready both the machinery and the facts to hit back hard and instantly if the media suddenly throw you onto the back foot.

The first of these is harder to organise; almost by definition, the news stories that cause problems to any organisation are the ones that cannot be anticipated. In many such situations a captain of industry or a Cabinet Minister is caught off guard over something that a key person in their organisation had known about and should have passed up the line. But by the time the media are in full cry, it is too late for any subordinate to say: 'By the way, there was something else I should have told you.' Only clear lines of commu-nication and a strong corporate culture can minimise the chance of this happening. Rebuttal is always second-best to the story not having appeared in the first place, as some mud will inevitably stick.

What do you do if you wake up to find that some highly damaging story for you has come out of nowhere and is dominating the headlines? First, you need to find out exactly what is being said: if you respond to allegations you have only heard second-hand, you may misunderstand the charges against you and make matters worse. Second, you need to check as fast as possible with the relevant people in your organisation whether the story is true or not. If it is false and the programme that carried the report is still being broadcast, you have no time to waste. You or your representative should get straight on to the producer, point out the error and demand a correction before the programme goes off the air. If the error is significant enough, they will comply.

The problem with any damaging story, whether true or not, is that once one news medium has carried it, it will 'grow legs'. Newspapers, radio and television stations will both repeat the story and follow it up, soliciting comments on it from people who may well include your enemies and then trying to ascertain further compromising facts. Just suppose that on a breakfast news programme you have been accused of despoiling the Brazilian rain-forest by having a desk made of mahogany from the region. By mid-morning, every environmental group the media can reach will be calling for sanctions against your organisation, and your political adversaries will be demanding your resignation. Without swift and effective intervention on your part, the story will run and run, and your reputation, your career or your share price will suffer long-term damage.

Time is of the essence, but you cannot begin your fightback without ammunition – hence the advisability of having the machinery in place to marshal your own facts and determine how they can most effectively be deployed. The political parties and other high-profile organisations now use specialised computer programs – such as Excalibur, of which the Labour Party made early use – which can pull out within moments past media reports that cover the subject in hand, and in particular the other parties' records on the issue. In a smaller organisation that is likely to attract controversy but lacks such resources, one member of staff should be tasked with pulling together the facts at short notice should some crisis with the media arise.

What facts do you need if you find yourself accused of planning the slaughter of the first-born? First of all, you need to ascertain whether what you are accused of is what you are actually planning to do. If it isn't, rebuttal on your part will consist of getting the original report corrected and ringing rapidly round the rest of the media to make sure they know the story is wrong and don't take it any further. This may be quite a challenge, as your denial will be seen by newsroom conspiracy theorists as a cynical attempt to suppress the truth. So the more supporting evidence you can rally, the better. In the interests of speed, it makes sense after taking issue with the original source of the story for you to ring the Press Association news agency and give them a statement categorically denying the story and giving your side of it. This will then be circulated in story form to newspaper offices and broadcasting organisations around the country, reducing the risk of some journalist who has heard the story on their way into work getting a follow-up into their own paper or bulletin before you have had a chance to rebut it. It won't kill the story, but it will at least make sure your side of it is given and may take some of the heat out of the situation. If a story is bad enough for you to have started the process of rebuttal, you should also make sure that you, or someone you can trust, are available to go and argue your case on radio and television until it has been fully heard. If you can't be bothered to do this, why should you be believed?

A flat denial is the simplest form of rebuttal. The real problem arises if the story you are faced with contains some degree of truth, or worse still is entirely accurate but has had a damaging construction placed upon it. Then you not only need to move fast to rebut it; you also have to have a credible line to explain and justify what you are doing. If you know the story is even partly true, do not attempt to deny it point-blank; you will simply be digging a deeper hole for yourself.

There are several lines you can take if confronted with an unwelcome but at least partly truthful story. If it still contains major inaccuracies, you can zero in on these and hope to discredit the entire story. This is a risky strategy, though, for you have to be careful not simply to look as if you are confirming the veracity of the rest of it. I remember a senior politician complaining that of ten charges levelled against his party by its opponents, three were untrue and two only partially true; he would have done better to say nothing. The best rule of thumb is that if the thrust of the story is accurate, you should make clear that your denial is a qualified one.

In such circumstances, you need to put together speedily a justification of what you are doing. On the back of this, you can then knock down those elements of the story that are untrue. For a start, you would presumably not be taking a certain course of action unless you thought it was the right and sensible thing to do. You need to isolate your most powerful reasons and communicate them as quickly and as forcibly as possible to the media. If you are doing something reluctantly, explain why you have been left with no real alternative. If your decision or course of action that has been brought to the public's attention has few redeeming features, you can try feeding the media a positive story about something slightly different; the more you can change the terms of the debate and get it on to your ground, the closer you are to getting off the hook.

If you are criticised by your political opponents for your course of action, it is handy if you can produce past quotes from them proposing precisely the same thing. And if you are accused of failing to consult, find people whom you have consulted. All too often, the people or groups who complain of not being consulted really mean a minority didn't get its way: one of the greatest headaches for any big business or organisation is that on many issues it will be confronted by small protest groups who are convinced that their view should prevail simply because of the strength of their feelings. You will never win them over, and it is usually a waste of time arguing with them. But you have to do enough to persuade ordinary, rational people that you are not riding roughshod over objectors with a real case and wide popular support.

If the media have got you bang to rights, there is one more form of rebuttal that may work for you if you are quick and brazen enough: attack. It's a gamble, but it may be the best chance you have. Remember how the Conservative Government treated the report of Sir Richard Scott's judicial inquiry into charges that Ministers had connived at breaches of military sanctions against Iraq: they attacked the Labour opposition for having called for the inquiry in the first place, and stuck to that line until the heat went out of the situation. It worked. And provided you can put together some ammunition or line up some accusations quickly enough and keep repeating them whatever questions the media or your opponents ask, you may get away with it. After all, their credibility is on the line as well as yours.

Rebuttal will not always lead to your point of view prevailing, but its speedy application can halt an inaccurate story in its tracks or persuade the media to modify the line being taken. Don't be put off by producers or news editors accusing you of strong-arm tactics; if they are reporting on the affairs of your company or organisation, their viewers, listeners and readers are entitled to know your point of view. But when you do make that crucial call to rebut a story, keep your cool. Be firm but factual, not objectionable. It may be hard to keep your temper if some irresponsible journalist or campaigner is threatening your own or your organisation's future, but if you can get your case across in this extremely difficult climate, the dividends are enormous.

Leaks

There are times when you want to get some subject raised in the media without identifying yourself with it: 'flying a kite' to see how the public will react to some idea before you formally launch it, or 'whistleblowing' to halt some practice of which you believe they will disapprove. In either circumstance, you may be tempted to leak.

Journalists love leaks. Leaks give them access to material that would otherwise be denied them, give them a feeling of one-upmanship over rivals who were not fed the information, and have a cloak-and-dagger mystique about them even if nothing legally or morally suspect took place. Even in these days of Freedom of Information, the best stories invariably come from leaks. But should you do it? The general rule is 'don't'.

The formal definition of leaking is the unauthorised disclosure of information to a journalist for use. On the other hand, if the information is yours to release, you can sometimes make a far greater impact by putting it out informally to one single journalist who is likely to give it a good show, rather than distributing the same information officially to everyone. Timing is often the main consideration. If you are going to make a big announcement, it may well be worth trailing it with one news organisation a few days before. The reporter gets a story, and you get an idea of how the announcement will play; if the public reaction is adverse, you can refine what you were planning to say.

Before giving any information informally to the media, you should ask yourself whether it is ethical or legal for you to make the call; if you are the company chairman, it probably is, provided the information is not market-sensitive – if you are the office junior, probably not. If you are in a subordinate position, you need to have uncovered some quite serious example of wrongdoing to be justified in blowing the whistle. The fact that you disapprove isn't enough: it may just show that you have gone to work for the wrong company, and most organisations these days have complaints machinery you are contractually obliged to go through.

The leak is such an effective weapon that I have even known PR professionals to dress up a story to look like a leak even when it wasn't, to heighten the impact. One party spokesman at the European Parliament consistently failed to get an extremely boring press release into the papers, so he stamped 'Secret' all over it and posted it under plain cover to the *Sunday Telegraph* – who printed it on their front page.

Combating a leak is something very different, and frequently demands instant and massive rebuttal. But before you say a word to the media in response to the leak, you need to have your strategy worked out. For a start, the moment you admit that there has been a leak and launch an investigation into how the information got out, you are conceding that the substance of it is true. The Ministry of Defence realised this some time ago, and now dismisses many leaks with the rejoinder that since the story is wrong, no leak can have taken place. (This is harder to do if the media have acquired an authentic document.) And if you are not admitting there has been a leak, self-evidently you cannot discipline the leaker.

Next you must ask yourself whether the way in which the leaked information has been presented requires you to rethink the policy in question while you still have the time. Occasionally a company, party or organisation realises how its proposed actions will play with the public only when they are leaked and the media turns instantly against them; even if the criticism is grossly unfair, it is worth considering a change of tack. You can then put your hand on your heart and say this was something people in your organisation were thinking of doing, but the idea has now been abandoned . . . If you do that quickly enough, you can leave the media with egg on their face for apparently getting the story wrong.

But if the leak is accurate and you wish to proceed with the strategy in question, you have just two choices: either to mount the strongest possible PR offensive to demonstrate the rightness and advantages of your actions (if necessary calling an instant press conference to highlight the benefits and take the high ground), or man your bunker and go for all-out rebuttal.

Should I complain?

If you don't like the coverage you receive, you should count to ten before blowing a fuse and ringing the reporter – or their editor – to complain. You need to ask yourself: 'is it the tone of the reporting that I don't like or has the journalist actually got the facts wrong?' Unless you have been seriously misrepresented, there is little point in complaining to any news organisation because you don't like how the story has come out; you will only make yourself look worse. Take this example from the *Shropshire Star*:

> *We have been asked to point out that Mary Magill was not having sex with a client when police raided premises in Wellington, as reported. She was in fact engaged in sexual activities.*

Ms Magill would have been wiser to let the matter rest.

Yet if what appears in print or on the air is grossly inaccurate or unfair, or if you are certain you have been misquoted, you should insist on a correction. Send a fax to the organisation responsible, rng them to say it's coming – and keep a copy in case you hear nothing back from them.

If there are genuine errors of fact, you should certainly make sure they are remedied. You agreed to the interview so that your point of view could be put across, and pointing out a mistake will both get the correct facts into the public eye and keep the journalist responsible on their mettle. Just as important, once an article containing an incorrect fact gets into a newspaper cuttings library or retrieval system, every journalist who writes or broadcasts about the subject in future is likely to repeat the mistake. So you should not only (politely) demand a correction, but also request that the news organisation's cuttings files or electronic library entries are either amended or tagged to show that a mistake was made. This will normally be done.

Some papers make a virtue of carrying a 'corrections' column. But don't expect the correction to be carried as prominently as the original story; it won't be. The broadcast media, and increasingly the press, do accept a responsibility to correct mistakes, but you can't expect them to do it with a flourish of trumpets. A mistake in a television or radio programme can be corrected almost instantaneously if the programme is live and you can persuade the production team that it matters enough – if, for example, they have got the date or venue of an event wrong. But mistakes or questionable statements in any programme recorded in advance, such as a documentary, can take ages to rectify, especially if you have to go through the full panoply of the statutory complaints machinery. Sometimes a solicitor's letter can concentrate minds and bring things to a head, but you should never actually threaten litigation unless you have the cash and the tenacity, not to mention a solid enough case, to be sure you want to go down that road.

Of course, not every erroneous statement in the media stems from an interview with the individual who is the subject of the mistake. A high proportion of factual errors concern people who aren't central to the story, yet these can still be very damaging – and often they concern peripheral points that a reporter has failed to check. The most obvious, and one of the most frequent, is the 'killing off' of some person still very much alive in a story that isn't really about them. In 15 years at the *Daily Telegraph*, I lost count of the number of times that colleagues killed off the designer Sir Cecil Beaton, the footballer Tommy Lawton and the musician Max Jaffa – and almost invariably the mistake came about when they were not the focus of the story. There would be a story about, say, the violinist Jack Smith, 'who played at the Scarborough Winter Gardens under the baton of the late Max Jaffa', and boom – in came a letter of complaint from an understandably furious Jaffa, and another magnum of Bollinger was on the way to the complainant, conveyed by the most glamorous female reporter available. Never expect money in compensation for errors in the media unless you have suffered pecuniary loss as a result, but if you have a taste for flowers or good champagne, you will be in luck. The most important remedy, however, is that 'tag' on your files in the cuttings library or electronic retrieval system to the effect that such a statement must never be repeated. The problem with the Beaton, Lawton and Jaffa stories, though, was that the notion that each had died was so deep in the reporter's subconscious that he or she had not bothered to check the cuttings. Lapses of this kind simply cannot be legislated against.

Another common cause of errors in newspapers is mishearings over the telephone. It is terribly important if you are using names, addresses, proper words or technical terms in a telephone interview that you check that the reporter knows how to spell them. Few such errors qualify for a correction, though I do remember one paper having to apologise for stating that the wedding reception was to be held 'at the home of the bride's father' rather than 'at the Old Manse.' On rare occasions they can be downright libellous: in my early days at the *Telegraph* we were forced to run an immediate correction stating that the newly elected President of the Oxford Union had worked as a navvy in the university vacation and was not, as had been stated due to a mishearing over the telephone, a former Nazi.

Some such errors occur without any involvement from the person being interviewed or written about; they arise because of a mishearing by one of the copytakers in the newspaper office, to whom stories are dictated by reporters in the field. Newspapers make less use of copytakers now that reporters can plug a laptop into a telephone socket and file their stories straight into the editorial computer, but the procedure still exists; most national newspapers now rely on a single squad of copytakers employed by the Press Association at Wetherby. Copytakers' mistakes are rare because they are highly proficient. When they do occur they can be highly amusing, such as the *Yorkshire Post* theatrical review which was headed 'A Doll's House, by Henry Gibson'.

Whenever you or your organisation or cause is referred to erroneously in print, you need to decide quickly whether it is worth your seeking to get the reference put right. You should ask yourself: 'Does it really matter?' and 'Could asking for a correction rebound on me?' (Never forget the war hero who was referred to as a result of a misprint as a 'battle-scared warrior'; a correction was sought, and in it he was branded a 'bottle-scarred warrior'.) And always remember, as Mr Pooter discovered in *Diary of a Nobody*, that over-insistence makes you look pompous.

But you should also consider whether seeking a correction gives you an opportunity to get more of your case across. Most editors dislike carrying items baldly correcting a mistake, but if you can offer them what looks like a new story with a correcting sentence buried in the text, they may well find such an article worth using on its merits.

One course open to you, whether the error is a minor or a serious one, is to write a letter to the editor pointing out the mistake, with a view to its publication; this can be a useful course to follow, particularly if the error is one you can be funny about. Remember Mark Twain on reading his own obituary: 'Reports of my death have been greatly exaggerated.' And frequently with a serious mistake, an editor would rather print a letter than a correction.

Should a media mistake – or deliberate statement – be really damaging, you may of course consider suing for libel. The general advice is: don't. It's expensive, you may very well lose, and unless your case is absolutely copper-bottomed and your own life history saintly you will probably come out with your reputation in tatters. It may seem outrageous to you that a tabloid has accused you of having oral sex with your partner in a Range Rover, but even if you haven't, count at least to a hundred before firing off that writ. The moment the whole sordid story is dissected in court, people who were never aware of the original libel will be slavering over its repetition in graphic detail. And never forget: no matter how highly you think of yourself, there may be people out there with a rather different view – and suing for libel gives them their day in the media spotlight.

2   Getting your story into print

Despite the advance of the electronic media, most people in this country still get the bulk of their news from the newspapers, national, regional and local. The average national newspaper can cover at least ten times as many stories as the radio or television news, and in more detail. So if you have a story to tell or a cause, event or business venture to publicise, it generally makes sense to go to the papers first, whatever else you do.

Having so much more space to fill, newspapers – particularly at national and regional level – have far larger news-gathering staffs. There is thus more chance of a call or tip-off from a member of the public being followed up in the first place. For this same reason, you are far more likely to be approached by a newspaper reporter than by a journalist from television or radio, though this is starting to change a little. Newspapers depend on contact with the public, who, after all, are their customers, for reader involvement sells papers; television, by contrast, is a top-down medium where the viewers are seen largely as an audience. This is reflected in the differing complaints machineries for the written and electronic media: the Press Complaints Commission deals largely with allegations of harassment of celebrities and members of the public by overzealous newspapers, while the Broadcasting Standards Commission and the Radio Authority monitor complaints about the fairness and quality of what the public see and hear.

Newspapers have one big advantage over radio and television that helps any member of the public with something to publicise: the reporter doesn't actually have to come to see you, though a good one with time on his or her side will try. Simply by asking you questions over the telephone, a newspaper reporter can gain all the information he or she needs for a perfectly respectable story, but that won't be enough for radio or television. A local radio station will settle, at a push, for a crackly telephone interview around which the reporter will tell the story, but it lacks the broadcast quality of a one-on-one with the reporter present and the interviewee speaking into a Uher or a Dat (the two main types of portable recorder). And television actively shies away from news items hinging on a telephone interview – unless it's some dramatic air–sea rescue at night, when the local coastguard controller or lifeboat coxswain comes into his own. If a story is big enough, every news organisation – press, radio and television – will send reporters with whatever electronic back-up is necessary. But for probably 95 per cent of news events, the newspapers have the edge for this reason.

The electronic media also shy away from news items where there is nothing to see or hear. One nightmare for television is the monthly trade figures: beyond graphics of cranes and containers there's absolutely no way of illustrating them, so increasingly news bulletins don't bother, even if the news is very bad. Newspapers have the same problem, too, though less severely. To make a page look interesting, several of the stories on it need to be illustrated with photographs. There is generally room for other items that do not lend themselves readily to such treatment, but a story accompanied by pictures always stands a better chance of being used, and some subjects are less photogenic than others. Articles about education are a particular nightmare because one classroom shot looks very like another, unless it's in a local paper when there is the hope of the children's parents buying the paper and maybe ordering prints of the picture. But if you are doing something that simply doesn't lend itself to pictures or give rise to the sound effects that so delight radio producers, the papers are the medium to aim for.

How newspapers work – and how to make the most of it

There are four types of newspaper in the UK: morning, evening, Sunday and weekly; their coverage is variously national, regional and local. If you have a story to tell, you need to decide which type of paper or combination thereof will suit your purpose best: for instance, you could decide to go to a national morning, your regional Sunday (if you have one) and your local weekly about aspects of the same story. You have two criteria to consider: is your story one that would appeal to the readership of that paper, and if the story is carried, can it appear at a time that will help you?

If you get this decision wrong, you will either gain no publicity at all or miss the bulk of your potential audience. There is no point in trying to go to a national daily with details of a cat show unless something quite exceptional is happening, but people still do. Equally, a story with strong human or political interest may well merit coverage in a national daily rather than a local weekly, even though such a paper might do the job with flair and even achieve results – such as the *Matlock Mercury*'s successful 27-year campaign to free Stephen Downing, a local man who had stayed in jail long after he could have been paroled to protest his innocence of a murder charge.

In choosing your newspaper you also need to make sure that it will be, if not necessarily sympathetic to your case, certainly not biased against it. Television and radio have no partisan slant, though they can be provocative. But some newspapers do, and it's important if your story is sensitive or political to go to one that is at best sympathetic or, failing that, neutral. For instance, if you're launching a Europe Week, there's no point in going to a Eurosceptic paper like the *Sun*; a paper that isn't sure we should be in Europe will at best not cover the event, or at worst use it as a pretext to rubbish your point of view. In that case you would have been better off not trying. Equally, if your business is trying to do something that is environmentally controversial and your local paper has a record of crusading on 'green' issues, you will at least have to take great care in how you put your story over. Not all editors are interested in listening to reason, and on many environmental and safety issues a shrill headline over an irresponsible story is far easier to run with than a genuinely informative article. Going to them with positive story A may simply prompt them to rush into print with negative story B, which they might otherwise not have considered.

On timing, the issue is a simple one of practicality. If you are organising an event or trying to prevent a decision being taken, there is no point in contacting a paper that will not appear until after the event or too shortly beforehand to make an impact. You also need to be aware of certain rhythms in the newspaper industry: most local weeklies appear toward the end of the week, generally Thursday or Friday, and most of their pages go to press a good 36 hours beforehand. An increasing number of evening papers, including the largest, the London *Evening Standard*, have stopped appearing on Saturdays when there are few commuters around – save for, in some cases, a sports edition with no significant news content. And most Sunday newspapers will carry only the most urgent stories that reach them on a Saturday.

Every morning in newspaper offices up and down the country, an editorial conference decides what stories are going to be used, and there are almost always more stories on the daily list than there will be room for – not to mention those that break later in the day or the week and elbow out the original candidates. At this conference, the news editor will list and explain his or her strongest runners for the day, the features editor ditto (most features pages are planned several days in advance, even on a daily paper), the picture editor will say where the paper's photographers are being sent and explain which stories offer the best opportunities for an unforgettable photo, and the sports and business editors will set out their agendas. Most important, the editor at the head of the table will exercise an arbitrary right of life or death over which stories are candidates to make the paper. Catch the imagination of this conference and you're halfway there. So you need to make sure the journalist you have spoken to is well aware of just why your story is special; in that way its full flavour can be presented to the editorial conference by the news, features or picture editor and it won't receive the thumbs down.

As the day or the week goes on, a paper's agenda changes as new stories break and some of those being researched turn out not to be quite as special as they seemed or appear in other arms of the media (a problem for the Sunday papers in particular; many good stories simply don't keep till the weekend). And as the deadline for each page – and eventually the paper as a whole – draws nearer, the chief sub-editor will allocate space to stories that have been written, and to pictures that may have news copy to accompany them, or maybe just a caption. (It is worth remembering that a handful of words in a caption to an eye-catching picture can have as much impact with the readers as a weighty story.) By early evening for a daily, mid-morning for an evening paper or Saturday lunchtime for a Sunday, just a few slots will remain for the most interesting stories; the remainder will either be 'spiked' (thrown in the electronic bin) or 'held over' for use in a subsequent edition. If your story hasn't appeared, it is worth ringing your journalist to let him or her know that it is suitable for reuse; if you can update it with fresh facts, it is well worth mentioning this provided they make a real difference. If the paper simply isn't interested, you are perfectly at liberty to try and place the story somewhere else, but out of courtesy you should tell your original target that you are looking elsewhere.

For the record, new technology has not given the papers later deadlines. The move away from printing processes dating back to Caxton, which offered hope of really late news getting into the papers, coincided with the accountants taking over, with their belief – not entirely unfounded – that the content and the immediacy of a paper are noticed only by the people writing for it. So don't leave it to the last minute to phone in your story; unless it is of earth-shattering importance, you will have missed your opportunity.

Sheer news value and scope for pictures don't alone determine what gets into the papers and what doesn't. One determinant is balance: there is a limit to the number of stories on the same subject, be it drugs, Europe or animals, that any paper will run in the same edition, even if it is running a campaign on the issue. Another is the availability of space and the amount of competition from other stories. How much space a paper allocates for news depends in the first instance not on how busy a news day (or week) it is, but on how much advertising space has been sold. This explains why the papers are fat in the run-up to Christmas, when all the shops are advertising, and thin in the summer holiday season, when they are not; by chance, those are also busy and slack periods respectively for news. With most papers, the allocation of space is a commercial rather than a journalistic consideration; indeed, at peak times for advertising, the amount of news space may actually be squeezed if the paper has reached the maximum size the printing plant can cope with. No newspaper management wants to turn advertisers away.

You can identify times of the year and the week when – assuming you have any choice in the matter – your story has a better chance of getting in. The volume of national, regional and local news abates considerably when Parliament and the courts aren't sitting – which in practice means Christmas and the ten days or so after, a week or so either side of Easter whenever it falls, and late July, August and late September; the Scottish Parliament is in recess throughout July. It is easier to get your story into print at these times, but you should also remember that during holiday periods many of the readers you want to target will be away.

Sunday's and Monday's papers are also usually easier to get a story into, simply because less of news value happens over the weekend – many a news editor with a blank schedule at lunchtime on Sunday has yearned for a really spectacular bus crash. Your chance of securing space on such a slack news day will be all the greater if you make contact halfway through the previous week, enabling the story to be written and planned in before the weekend break begins. However, your success can never be guaranteed: I was duty editorial writer for the *Sun* the day Princess Diana was killed, and I saw many stories that would otherwise grab the headlines bite the dust through no fault of their own. Yours could have been among them.

If the issue you want to promote is not time-sensitive, it is worth keeping an eye on the news in case an opportunity appears for your story to piggyback on national coverage of your special subject. There are times when the press become preoccupied with, say, child welfare, global warming or law and order; and if your story is relevant, it may become much easier to interest your local or regional paper in it – or to get a national paper to take it up as a further example of the trend already being reported. To give an example: circa 1969 there was a rash of stories about British Rail losing holidaymakers' dogs, and for a time any story in this vein was guaranteed a spot in the tabloids. In isolation, none would have made much of an impact, but when they were put together they were a PR disaster for the railways. (Doubly so when, in a story I covered, the press were called to the station to see a boy lovingly reunited with a dog he had never seen before in his life.) On a more serious note, the *Daily Mail* has put together powerful double-page spreads on, for example, multiple instances of illegal immigrants with HIV having to be treated in Britain by the NHS because no airline would fly them home. The impact of several cases is always greater than of one isolated incidence, because there is a common theme.

It is also worth keeping up with the news just in case something happens that invalidates your story or obliges you to rethink it. There is nothing worse than getting on to a newspaper saying that you have just heard the first cuckoo of spring, to be told that someone else reported it yesterday.

Community activists sometimes ask if it's worth writing the story themselves and submitting it to the paper rather than talking it through with a reporter. There is no harm in setting out your case on paper – indeed that's pretty much what a press release is (see Chapter 6). But unless you are targeting a local paper or free sheet which you know has a tiny editorial staff, you should always expect the reporter to want to set out the story in his or her own words. This is partly because it's their training and their job to do this, bringing out clearly the points they reckon the readers will find most interesting, but also because it's very difficult for even well-educated members of the public to write with the tightness and economy of words that most newspapers in this country require. Unlike the press in America – which take themselves very seriously, have oceans of space and cannot tell the time without explaining how the clock was invented – even today's large papers in Britain have never quite lost the economy of words that was forced on them in the years of wartime newsprint rationing and the union-imposed limitations on newspaper size which lasted well into the 1970s. Even though you could now insulate your loft with the *Sunday Times*, read it carefully and you will still find it tightly written.

If you want to make absolutely sure that advance notice of your jumble sale, dog show or protest meeting does get into the papers or that the decisions taken by your organisation are put on record, there is always the last resort of taking out advertising space. Display advertisements in local newspapers, at least, are not expensive, and provided the content isn't at all provocative most papers are delighted to carry them. This procedure should be only a last resort if you have been unable to tickle the paper's editorial palate, as it is obviously preferable to get your publicity *gratis*, but it may prove inevitable. Zambian Ministers whom I media-trained confessed to me that they were unable to get important decisions they took into the papers even though most of them were owned by the Government, and had to resort to taking out adverts. Indeed, advertising forms an important and costly part of our own Government's media strategy. It would be impossible through the news columns alone to campaign effectively for home or road safety, to get people to pay their taxes on time or to maximise take-up of social security benefits – it is newspaper and television advertising that gets the best results.

The three things you have to assess in taking out an advertisement are:

- Will the cost of the advert be money well spent?
- Is the periodical you are advertising in the one most likely to be read by the people you want to reach?
- If you are giving advance notice of some event, are you timing it right? I once inserted an advert for a forthcoming dance in my

local weekly nine days before it was due to take place, rather than two, and the results were pathetic. Too far ahead and people will forget; give them too little notice and they won't have time to clear their diaries.

Every picture tells a story

In deciding how you can grab a paper's attention for your story or event, you should always think pictures. If you can create the opportunity for a memorable photo, you will stand a much better chance of getting your story into the paper, and of getting it noticed. And if the picture is an action shot, there's a real chance that local television, at least, may be interested.

Newspaper photographs, with rare exceptions, used to look dreadful. Picture quality under the old hot-metal process was appalling, and the composition settled for by too many papers was turgid in the extreme. The advent first of television and then of web-offset printing forced newspapers to improve it. Pictures no longer looked as if they had been taken through an old sock, and press photographers were set the challenge of becoming more imaginative. Shots of groups of people with wine glasses in their hands or 'sharing a joke' simply wouldn't do any more – though you do still sometimes come across them. Nor – a message here for the public relations industry which still transgresses, as well as for community groups issuing a press release about some new appointee – are picture editors today interested in posed shots of a newly promoted business person with a phone clamped to their ear. A good picture can lift a story; a bad one can kill it.

Is there anything you are doing that would make a good picture? If not, could you stage one? Suppose you are campaigning for a pedestrian crossing at an accident blackspot. A shot of yourself with cars passing in the background would just about do, but if you organised a dozen mothers or children to parade with placards – or even, dare I say it, block the road – you would immediately be giving a photographer what they are looking for. And if you can get some local celebrity along to take part – providing they haven't done it too often before – your chances of finding a photographic peg for your story are all the brighter.

One note of caution. If you do block the road you should get the local police on your side so that they stop the protesters being run over and don't arrest them. There's a very narrow dividing line between a protest and a stunt, and there have been enough complaints over the years about television crews in Northern Ireland encouraging bored kids to throw rocks at the police for you to proceed with care. But you may even find the reporter who comes to cover your story suggesting that you ramp up the protest in the interest of getting not only headlines, but results. I've done it myself. In 1970 I organised a sit-in in the station master's office at Manchester Piccadilly after passengers on the very last train through the Woodhead tunnel from Sheffield arrived so late that they missed the final one back. A grubby engine and an even grubbier crew were located and an extra train put on – sparing from frostbite two hikers we picked up en route at a tiny Pennine station, unaware the train they had missed was meant to be the last one ever.

If you get a reporter interested in covering your story, it's well worth asking if he or she can bring a photographer. Press photographers make their living out of making the normal look exciting, and their imagination, experience and professionalism may well be able to conjure up a picture opportunity you haven't thought of. If you are dealing with a local paper, you will also quite often find that the photographer's local knowledge and even story sense is better than the reporter's; this is because photographers tend to move around less and are often a mine of experience. When I was on a local paper, the time spent on the drive out to a job being briefed by the photographer was invaluable.

There are certain things to watch if a photographer does turn up. Make sure before he/she starts shooting that you don't look scruffy (hair combed, flies done up, etc.). If you're a woman wearing a short skirt, don't let them shoot you getting out of your car (there are numerous samizdat shots of royal stocking-tops or worse tucked away in national picture desks). Equally, don't let them shoot you from below if you're wearing a billowing dress; the result can be embarrassing, particularly if you haven't got the legs or bum for it.

Above all, don't let them talk you into being pictured doing anything that could make you look ridiculous – if one of your colleagues doesn't mind losing their dignity, that's a matter for them. And if you've a friend with you, ask them to stand next to the photographer and make sure that what he or she can see in the lens is something you would be happy with.

Check the background too: you don't want to be pictured beneath or next to something that makes you look silly or detracts from your message. Any photographer worth his or her salt won't take a picture of you with a tree or telegraph pole growing out of the top of your head, but – particularly with a distance or group shot – something embarrassing can always creep into the picture. More than one business leader has been pictured against a backdrop reading 'Success after 50 years of failure', only to find when the picture was cropped for use in the paper their own mugshot with the word 'failure' above it: think of the message that conveys. And never forget William Hague who, just before the 2001 election, unwisely spoke on a foot-and-mouth visit with a pair of antlers mounted on the wall behind him. It took an ingenious snapper just seconds to line the two up and there, on the front page of the *Mirror* the next day, was

Hague with a pair of antlers growing out of his head and the inevitable headline 'Deer, Oh Deer'. His media 'minder' that day should have been culled along with all those infected sheep.

Above all, if a photographer turns up to your event, make sure he or she knows who everybody is. A good press photographer (and most are) makes a point of writing down everyone's name, checking unusual spellings and ascertaining useful facts for the picture caption, such as who is a parish councillor and who is chair of the parents' committee. Indeed, most reporters who come out on jobs of this kind rely on the photographer to confirm that they have got these facts right. But you need to check: more than once I have got back to the office and realised I didn't know who one or more of the key participants was – or, even more seriously, I thought I knew and was wrong. It is in your interest to make sure the paper has all the facts it needs.

Most press photographers are fine ambassadors for their newspaper. As such, they may very well ask you if you would like a copy of one of the pictures they have taken – especially if your children are in it. If they don't, you can usually buy prints from the paper's photographic sales department, and they're not that expensive. Increasingly a press photographer will shoot film in both black-and-white and colour, so you may have a choice. (Which the paper uses depends on the page selected for the story; unless a paper is in full colour, only certain pairs of pages will be in colour, with the rest in monochrome.)

Increasingly these days the photographer will turn up with a digital camera and if you are lucky he or she will show you the pictures they've taken. It's well worth asking if you can have a look – provided you don't start telling them their job.

It may seem the wrong way round to deal with pictures in the papers and your contact with the people who take them before getting on to discuss your relationship with the actual reporter. But in very many cases the story hangs on the picture, and not the other way round. If you read the average newspaper picture caption, there is often little pretence that any news event is connected with it – it's just that to produce an attractive page you need interesting pictures, and if they haven't got one of your angelic schoolkids blocking the road they will use one of Gwyneth Paltrow at a film première. Which is of more use to you?

The telephone interview

For most people, their first contact with a newspaper reporter will be on the telephone. Either you will have called their organisation in the hope of getting your story into the paper, or they will have heard about something that involves you and want to know more. If they make the call, you are quite within your rights, as I said earlier, to ask for a few minutes to get your thoughts and information together and then call them back. If you ring them, you should have the full facts at your fingertips so that you can run right through your story with them. It looks very bad if you can't.

The first thing you should do when a reporter rings is ask them who they are. A surprising number of people don't do this, and when things go wrong all they can remember is that 'someone from the *Argus*' rang them. Second, find out which part of the paper they are writing for: news, sport, business or features. And third, take down their number in case you need to ring them back.

You should ask them why they are ringing – amazingly some people don't do this either, and get sucked into a conversation they would rather not have begun. And it's also worth asking them who else they have spoken to: that will give you some idea of how well they have already grasped the issue, and whether they have made contact with anyone who might be unhelpful or whose views you will need to explain or rebut.

When the interview gets under way – and this applies just as much face to face as over the phone – you need to *talk slowly and clearly* so that the reporter can write everything down – even a good shorthand writer will struggle to keep up with normal conversation. Spell out any names he or she may not be familiar with; people and places you deal with every day may be completely new to your interviewer. And it's worth checking that they're getting the spellings right; you have no means of telling how closely a reporter at the other end of the phone is paying attention. There are fewer distractions if he or she is sitting in your front room.

Answer one question at a time. You will give your best if you go at your own speed; if the reporter tries to bounce you by firing off a string of questions, take a deep breath and deal with the one you would prefer to answer. If the questions are hostile, the reporter is shooting himself in the foot by asking them all at once, as you have the opportunity to respond to the one you can most easily deal with. If you'd like to answer the others but he or she is simply going too fast, ask them to slow down.

Stick to the point. If you have a message to get across, you don't want to cloud the issue so that the reporter hangs up totally confused about the thrust of what you are trying to say. This may be the only chance you ever have to get across your point of view, so don't waffle or digress. The only exception is that if you don't particularly like the line of questioning the reporter is following, it's quite handy to veer away from it. But you can only take this tactic so far, as when the reporter sits down to write the article they can get the last word by saying you were evasive – and that will tell against you.

Perhaps most importantly, *don't say anything to the reporter that you wouldn't want to see in print.* The last thing you want is for some off-the-cuff remark from yourself, possibly about a completely different subject, to grab the headlines. If you know a reporter really well, you may be able to take them into your confidence, but unless and until you do, you shouldn't be tempted to go 'off the record' or, even worse, start gossiping. If you feel something needs explaining, though, you can ask the reporter to put their notebook down while you talk them through some technical point.

It is well worth the time and trouble to explain things a journalist may not understand, and if you get into complex areas you should ask if they are keeping up with you. It's frustrating for a reporter to realise post-interview that they haven't grasped some vital technical element of the story, and it's human nature in that situation for them to try and bluff their way through instead of ringing back and admitting they didn't understand what they were being told. By the same token, if you don't know or aren't sure of a fact and the reporter isn't up against a deadline, tell them you will call them back with it – and make sure you do.

It's very easy to let your guard down as an interview nears its end. Remember the cautionary tale of the late Nicholas Ridley, who had to resign as Trade and Industry Secretary after telling a journalist from the *Spectator* what he really thought about the Germans when he assumed the formal part of the conversation was over. The tape recorder was still running, and the comments caused a furore when they appeared in print. So until you have actually put down the telephone, remember there is a news-hungry journalist at the other end. If in doubt, say nowt.

If you feel the interview is dragging on or that you've said all there is to say, you can politely bring it to an end. Newspaper interviews last far longer then broadcast ones, and interviews in person – for instance, if you are interviewing the Prime Minister at Downing Street – will go on for longer than those done over the phone (forty minutes is my maximum). But you can cover an awful lot of ground in ten minutes, and unless you are dealing with a very important or highly complex matter, ten minutes on the phone should be quite enough.

Before you hang up, there are several things you should check. Would it help if the reporter came to see you in person (assuming you want them to)? Do they want to send a photographer? When is the article they are preparing likely to appear? The journalist who interviews you may not always know this, but if they do it is helpful not only in terms of making sure that you get to see the article (and can alert any friends or colleagues who may be interested) but also because, if the story is not for immediate use, you may be able to talk to the reporter again and give further assistance. And finally, double-check the reporter's name and number. Then sign off politely and let the reporter get on with the job of turning your words into a story.

Chequebook journalism

A lot of people fondly believe that even the most mundane news item is a saleable commodity. By and large, they are wrong. Newspapers – even the serious ones – will pay journalists in other parts of the media well, if not generously, for bringing interesting stories to their attention. And they will always reward even an amateur for a good picture – just think what the French lorry driver who shot the only film of the Concorde crash must have made. But one of the greatest turn-offs for any news desk is a call from some punter with a story of debatable interest who opens the conversation by talking money. Approach a newspaper that way, and you will be told to get lost.

If you are fortunate enough to come across one of the rare stories that can actually earn you megabucks, it may be worth asking the likes of Max Clifford to negotiate on your behalf. If you happen upon a celebrity or showbiz exclusive, there's a fair chance that several of the tabloids, not to mention *Hello!* and *OK!*, may be interested, and it makes sense for the story to go to the highest bidder. Organising an auction of this kind is something few people outside the media – or inside for that matter – have the aptitude or the taste for, and if your commodity is that marketable you would be crazy to do it yourself. An expert in this field will know which papers are most likely to be interested, how best to present the story to them and how to bid them up. At the same time, you will have to take their word for it if they don't reckon the story is in the big league, or if for some reason it simply isn't a runner. And you will also have to remember that the person staging the auction will want their cut.

Every journalist has come up with at least one exclusive story where he or she can just see the tabloid headlines, only to see it collapse. Maybe the story simply doesn't stand up; there may be some important fact you simply don't know – for instance, that the blonde you saw Star X locked in a clinch with is his long-standing but little-seen wife. Or the story may be just a little too near the knuckle. I once was told by a veterinary nurse how a male baboon brought into the surgery because it was oversexed had started making advances to the equally male vet, and had had to be restrained. I rushed to make contact with the *News of the World*, only to be told by a news editor: 'If only it had been a female baboon!' There are numerous examples of freelances ringing the *Sun* news desk with a lurid story just – or well – beyond the bounds of taste, who have been told: 'It's not one for us, old boy. Try the *Daily Star*.' And I imagine the *Daily Star* refers its raunchier callers to the *Daily Sport*.

The great days of chequebook journalism were in the 1950s, in the age of mass circulations and lavish editorial spending. Now that accountants have taken over the media, even the flashiest tabloids have limited budgets for 'buy-ups', and most of this cash seems to go to B-list celebrities who kiss and tell for the Sunday papers. The chance of a journalist bearing down on an unsuspecting member of the public waving a fistful of tenners is, I am sorry to say, very limited.

Nevertheless it does happen, and if you are offered money by a newspaper – maybe by some fixer or 'heavy' rather than a reporter pure and simple – there are some questions you need to ask yourself pretty rapidly. And the first and most important of these is: 'If I tell what I know, will my partner/parents/children/friends/neighbours/workmates ever speak to me again?' If the answer is 'No', you should then ask yourself: 'Would that matter?' If you can live with the stigma, go ahead and spill the beans. Equally, if you're happy to answer the question, don't volunteer to talk for nothing if the person approaching you looks as if they are going to offer you money. You should also take great care that the offer of money isn't the start of a slippery slope that leads to your doing something unethical or illegal, like hacking into a workmate's computer or rifling through his dustbin. Most journalists wouldn't dream of asking anyone to break the law – but there are a few who just might, particularly if they're under pressure from a demanding news desk haunted by the fear of another paper getting the story first, or in greater detail.

From my experience, all chequebook journalism by national newspapers these days has to be specifically approved by the editor or a very senior executive. Reporters simply aren't sent out with wads of cash as once some might have been. Payment for information falls into a very different league, but most reporters, even on the most ruthless papers, are sufficiently good at their job that they don't need to pay; they know how to wheedle information out of people free of charge. And if you ask them for money, they will simply go and get the facts from somebody else. Remember: the moment you turn story-getting into a commercial transaction, you destroy your own moral credibility. And you may even find yourself exposed in print. The woman who went to the *Sunday People* with photos of Princes William and Harry abseiling down a Welsh dam when in the care of Tiggy Legge-Bourke must have been mortified when the paper printed highly intimate details of her own past.

Privacy

Britain's newspapers, and in particular the tabloids, often come under fire for invasions of privacy. And it could be that your first contact with the media is when some overzealous photographer catches you sunbathing topless in your garden and sells the story to the *Sun* or *OK!*, or when you find that a reporter has been trawling through your dustbin in the hope of finding something incriminating in your bank statement. Both practices are highly reprehensible, and in the latter case illegal, but they do happen. And they have proved crucial to exposing serious cases of wrongdoing just often enough for some editors to turn a blind eye to the practice.

The two defences mounted by unscrupulous editors are that almost any conduct is justifiable if the activities of the person whose privacy is being invaded are worthy of exposure, and that any figure in the public eye has no right to privacy. Bullshit. If you find a snapper on the grassy knoll overlooking your garden or some dingy figure sorting through your wheelie bin, call the police. They may not prosecute, but they will find out who your unwelcome visitor is and whom they represent. Then you should ring the editor of the publication in question and play hell with them, threatening them with the Press Complaints Commission. The Commission is a shadowy organisation with few real powers, but most editors treat it with respect, and unless you have been caught stealing the Crown Jewels it is unlikely a paper that has violated your rights will wish to argue the toss with the PCC. And remember, the PCC will always back you if your school-age children are dragged into the headlines simply because you are important.

Frequently a newspaper will claim that the journalist who doorstepped you in an advanced state of intoxication is a freelance acting without their authority; this may be so, but it is also a standard excuse. It is, however, worth checking with the paper, before you go right off the deep end, whether or not the person you have apprehended is in fact a member of their staff – the really wily operator, when caught, may well claim to be working for another paper to cover his or her tracks and divert the blame.

If you do find that a reporter is invading your privacy, it is well worth asking why. They may well not be trying to snatch a photo of you because of your remarkable physique – they probably suspect you are up to something, and if you don't already know what you are supposed to have done you need to find out. And if you are in it up to your neck, this just could be the time for that call to Max Clifford, or, less dramatically, your solicitor.

Equally, it is essential if you find someone going through your dustbin or trying to tap into your bank or tax records that you ascertain, prontissimo, what story they are chasing. Again, there may be some allegation of malfeasance against you – quite possibly something of which you are totally unaware or which you never imagined would look reprehensible to anybody else. Or you may discover that your records are being trawled through in an attempt to expose some other person. You may wish to warn that person – or you may even be so scandalised by the story that is being unearthed that you feel like co-operating with the media yourself (though probably not with the paper that has invaded your privacy).

It is not uncommon for an individual who finds that the press are at work on a story concerning them to ring a more trustworthy paper and give them the full and real story. Sometimes you can even get your version into print first, and grab the moral high ground.

Non-news media

One very handy way of reaching your public or getting your case across is to harness the non-news media. Quite apart from the high-profile glossies like *Hello!* and the mass-circulation women's (and lads') magazines, there are hundreds of periodicals that specialise in everything from cars and computers to trout fishing and country pursuits. Between them their circulation is immense, and they are keenly read by members of the public who share that particular interest – so if that interest is yours or there is a product or issue you are eager to publicise, these magazines are a natural target for you. Even if you don't normally read them, it is easy to check out the display racks at your newsagent or pop into your local reference library and trawl through one of the regularly updated guides that list every periodical in the country to identify one or more whose readership could be responsive to your message.

The best proof of the importance of the non-news media is the way political image makers strive to cultivate them. Great effort is put by the parties into placing profiles and 'soft' interviews of their leaders with women's magazines, and into cultivating 'niche' publications ranging from *Saga* magazine, targeted at high-spending over-50s, to music, hobby and lifestyle magazines where a particular side of a politician can be displayed to a potentially empathetic audience. But if you are dealing with a magazine whose readers have a very different lifestyle from your own, don't try to strike up an artificial rapport: it may have seemed a bright idea for William Hague to have told *GQ* that he used to drink fourteen pints a day while working on a delivery truck for his father's soft drinks business, but the revelation merely left him looking silly.

Competition for editorial space in the most high-profile periodicals is immense; some of the mass-circulation magazines produced by the supermarkets for sale at checkouts contain only a couple of articles that are not about food or other products on offer, so the scope for getting into them is very limited. Equally, big-ticket women's magazines are strictly formulaic and most space in them is bagged by well-established freelance writers. So unless you happen to know someone writing in this field, trying to secure publicity in periodicals of this kind is well-nigh impossible. If you do find yourself in the glossies (and that includes the weekend newspaper supplements) the initial approach is most unlikely to have come from you; it will almost certainly have come from the publication itself after someone there has read about you, or more likely from a freelance who hopes to sell your story to them.

Specialist magazines tend to have rather more space, and to be more open to approaches from people who share that interest and have a story to tell. That does not mean they are in any way amateurish; their editorial team and production staff are likely to be highly proficient. Nor does it mean that they print many unsolicited articles: most such are rejected, and again there will be a favoured circle of freelances whose contributions are most likely to be used. Once you have made contact with your specialist magazine or weekly, the same process of feeding in the information will apply as if you are dealing with a newspaper – though if you share that magazine's interest you may have rather less to explain on the technical front. An approach to a specialist publication by a layperson with an interesting story to tell is very likely to be followed up. A phone call is always the best way because you know it has got through, and because you can enlarge on your message; faxes and e-mails to any office have a habit of getting lost or being ignored.

You should never submit an article or press release by e-mail and assume it has arrived in a form that makes sense to the recipient. All too often, in my experience, the person receiving the e-mail finds that they can't open the document attached, or that having opened it they are confronted by gibberish. They will seldom contact you to ask for it to be resent in a form they can read, and all your hard work is thus wasted. You can reduce this risk by sending any attachment as 'text', which can be read by almost any computer, but you still need to ring up and make that check, not least because some commissioning editors never bother to read either their own e-mail or copy submitted to them electronically.

3   Making an impact on television

Television is the most powerful medium of all, and a tremendous source of free publicity if you can harness it. Just thirty seconds on television can turn you into a star, work wonders for your business or the campaign you are trying to launch – or leave millions of people convinced you are a villain or, worse still, an idiot. People have consciously to buy newspapers, but television brings you straight into their homes, and they will form an instant judgement when they see you, often before you open your mouth.

Despite its power, television isn't a medium you should be frightened of. Everyone you see on the screen is a fellow human being with the same faculties as yourself, and if you act naturally and play to your strengths you can communicate your case to good effect. And in getting that case across, how you look is at least as important as what you say. If you look uneasy or unkempt or dress wrong for the medium or the occasion, people either won't remember your message or will take against it. Give a good impression, and you're halfway to winning the argument.

Television works very differently from the written press, not just in the obvious sense that it is an electronic medium, but because of the way it is structured. As I mentioned in the context of the complaints machinery, television is a top-down medium rather than a bottom-up one, with a much lower level of consumer involvement in the product than with newspapers. This doesn't mean that you can't gain airtime for your cause or project or that you can't blag your way onto the air. But what appears on the screen is firmly in the hands of schedulers, directors and producers, not to mention the advertisers, and there is simply less scope than with the written media to get your view across.

In addition, there is far less news coverage, both national and regional, on television – a much smaller proportion of the daily output, less scope within the time allocated for news to cover the range of stories a newspaper can deal with, and, at local level, simply far less television than newspapers, though purely community stations do exist.

Unless you have a story that would make the front page of a national paper, it is frankly not worth bothering to contact the BBC at national level or ITN; you would be better going straight to your regional station. At either level, if you do make contact, you should ask to speak to the news desk (or business or sports desk); the news/features distinction in newspapers is matched by a news/docu-mentaries divide in television, with 'fluffy' and heart-jerking items cropping up in the closing minutes of news bulletins, and much newsworthy material with no obvious 'peg' appearing in current affairs programmes and documentaries. These latter are hard to crack. Unless you know a television producer in this field, or a programme maker comes to you because your views or activities have attracted their interest, you will have no awareness of what documentaries are planned, and no means of getting a particular subject raised as you can with a newspaper or through broadcast news coverage.

Local television news in this country is dreadful by world standards – in terms of the amateurish way many bulletins are put together, the way the BBC, in particular, expects viewers from county A to regard news from county B a hundred miles away as 'local', and the extreme tameness and parochiality of 99 per cent of the items covered. Nevertheless, people watch it and if you are launching a campaign in your community it is a worthwhile medium to try – just don't mind if your name appears over a picture of a prominent royal or vice versa, as used to happen regularly to interviewees on the BBC's *Newsroom SouthEast*. Fortunately, the reporters on most regional news programmes are thoroughly professional and will give you a fair and sensible hearing; it's not their fault if things fall apart in the studio. And if you are dealing with a community cable television station, you will almost certainly find that the enthusiasm of the staff you deal with eclipses their expertise; the disadvantage for you here will be the tiny audience.

Regional television news coverage relies very heavily, as local newspapers do, on court cases, road accidents, community campaigns, the activities of local councils and the like. If you are trying, say, to save a local hospital or get a pedestrian crossing installed at an accident blackspot, this could be the medium for you. Your chances of getting onto the news are very much better if you can offer something worth filming, though do remember that if you try to take a television crew into the A&E department of your local hospital or a classroom in your local school, you – and they – are likely to get thrown out. But even if you can't get into the premises you are complaining about or are fighting to save, you can usually find a handy spot outside from which to make your case in a photogenic way: groups of protesting children may be a cliché, but to regional television news producers they are manna from heaven. By the same criterion, any story involving animals, the cuddlier the better, stands a very good chance of getting airtime: remember Phoenix, the calf who survived the foot-and-mouth cull?

Don't be surprised if, once you have interested the regional BBC or commercial television news team in your story, the reporter researches it over the telephone; most such stations are desperately short on camera crews and at the very least they will want (time permitting) to make sure the story merits sending one out before they arrange for anyone to come and see you. But if they do send a reporter with a crew, there is a very good chance that they will use the story. One note of caution: if the phone call starts sounding rather like a formal interview, you should double-check that this is simply a conversation to ascertain the facts and not being taped for use on the air.

Setting the terms

If a television programme of any kind contacts you with a view to your appearing, you should *ask yourself whether going on television will advance your case.* Don't panic and automatically say 'No' – this may be your golden opportunity.

If the story does put you in a bad light, they will run it anyway, whether you put your side of it or not. If you don't want to be interviewed, is there a statement you can make – in writing to the station or read by yourself or your representative to camera – that will make your point without giving them the chance to ask you awkward questions? And should your solicitor see it first, to make sure you aren't making things worse for yourself by falling into some legal elephant trap?

At the other extreme, no matter how confident you are, you shouldn't rush to get in front of the cameras without considering the difficulties. Not every television interviewer is a Jeremy Paxman who can fillet the toughest politicians; most just want to get to the facts and may even encourage you to tell your story. But if there is some killer question you know they might ask, stay off the air.

Even if your case is unanswerable, it is worth considering if there is someone you trust who could put the argument better, or who would look more lively or convincing in presenting it. If you are representing an organisation, you can afford to be tough about who you put up for a broadcast, particularly if it is a discussion, and who is put up against them: you don't see Cabinet Ministers going in to bat against back-bench MPs, nor do many chief executives agree to be grilled on television by one of their junior staff. If they are keen to have you on the programme, you have bargaining power: use it if you need to.

Yet if you are relaxed about going on television and feel you can put your case well, don't be bashful; you may be the person best qualified to put the argument. It may even be just the chance you have been waiting for to explain why, for instance, your local council should approve your plan to build a factory close to a beauty spot despite a vocal residents' campaign against it – or, indeed, why the factory should not be built even though it would bring badly needed jobs.

Before you agree to go on the air, there are several things you should establish – particularly if you have been invited to the television company's studio where you are to some extent at the mercy of their technology and their way of doing things. First of all, is it to be broadcast live? This isn't just important because if it's recorded you should be able to get home in time to see yourself on the telly. If your appearance is being recorded for later transmission, there is always the chance of being able to take a question again if you 'fluff' it or are not happy with the answer you are giving – and you will be perfectly within your rights to do so. If it is live, you will have just the one chance to get it right – occasionally you see interviewees ask for a retake when on live, and it makes them look very stupid. And don't forget, on television you can't (unless you are sitting behind a desk) carry any kind of prompt card to remind you of the points you want to make; you have to rely on your memory.

You also need to find out about the format. Is it a straightforward interview, one-on-one with the reporter or presenter? Or is it a broader discussion, and if so, who are the other participants going to be? Are they just coming to interview you, or will they be talking to other people, and if so, who? The vaguer the producer planning the programme is with you about who the other participants will be, the more likely they are to insert at the last minute someone you know would give you a hard time or knock down your arguments after you have spoken. If that stunt is pulled on you (and I have seen it done at the highest level in television), you have every right to withdraw from the programme – but don't forget that those who do take part will then be free to rubbish you. Remember the impact of Paul Merton appearing on *Have I Got News for You* with a tub of lard in the seat next to him after Roy Hattersley failed to appear? The time to get the question of who is participating sorted out is well before you go on the air.

Equally, if a reporter is coming to see you, find out if they are doing a news 'package' and, if so, who else will be on it. You can't tell the television company who they should interview, but if your arch-enemy is going to be on the programme it is worth knowing in advance, so that you can deal in the most effective way with the points they are likely to raise. Knowing who else is being interviewed will give you a fair idea of the shape of the story they hope to run. It is also important to know how long you are likely to be on the air for. Don't be insulted if they say two or three minutes; you can say an awful lot in that time. But the shorter the interview is likely to be, the fewer points you will have a chance to raise and explain.

You also need to find out if there will be a studio audience. For current affairs and discussion programmes, there often will be, and a live audience on your side can be a very useful weapon in convincing people at home. If you do have a studio audience, you can usually get a laugh or applause out of all but the most hostile members if you pitch right your handling of the questions – and your handling of the other panellists. But equally, if you are defending an unpopular cause or your opponents are able to 'pack' the audience, the whole thing can turn nasty. Every television current affairs producer wants a lively audience as it makes the broadcast go with a fizz, but if the participants get out of control it can wreck the programme or do you and your cause serious harm. So you should always check with the producer as to who is supposed to be in the audience, who they are representing, how they were selected and what their role in the programme is supposed to be. If you are on television to debate a controversial issue, you need to be certain that your opponents will not dominate the audience or that you have as many supporters in the studio as you need. You should also think twice about taking part in live programmes with audience participation. With a pre-recorded programme, the producer can always halt the proceedings, remove anyone who is causing trouble, and lower the temperature; with a live programme, especially on the BBC where there is no scope for an extra commercial break if things in the studio get out of hand, anyone staging a stunt is guaranteed an audience of millions.

There are other things you need to know when you are discussing arrangements for the programme. What precisely is it about? (Strangely, some people go on to the air without even having found this out, with disastrous results.) And what will the line of questioning be – or at the very least the first question? You will seldom get an interviewer to tell you all their questions beforehand, even if they are sympathetic: a broadcast interview is a living thing and the second question will sound fresher if it follows on from your answer to the first. But if you know the opening question, you can at least have one answer reasonably well prepared – and make sure it includes your soundbite, of which more later.

If the television crew is coming to you, should they come to your home, to your workplace or the premises of your organisation? Is there somewhere you could take them to that would make a good backdrop for television? When do they want to come? Is that time convenient to you? Will there be strong daylight or will they need to bring their own lighting? (They may need both.) And how many of them will there be?

If you are going onto a discussion or current affairs programme rather than the news, you should ask whether and how much you are being paid; it's bad form to ask a newspaper this, but when you are asked to appear on television as public entertainment you are entirely within your rights. And if you are going to their studio, make sure they organise a cab for you – and give you the cab firm's number in case it doesn't turn up.

No matter what kind of programme you are appearing on or where you are doing it, there are certain basic things you can do beforehand to increase your impact, or at least make sure you don't undersell yourself.

First, your appearance and dress. You want to make an impact without terrifying or distracting your audience. Violent colours, big hair, dangly earrings, plunging necklines will all take the viewer's mind off what you are trying to say: avoid them. Busy checks and stripes will shimmer on the television screen and tempt people watching at home to switch over to something less stressful; white garments are simply too bright for the camera and will cause it to 'strobe', which is just as irritating. Your best bet is to dress simply but smartly, in mildly contrasting colours, so that what you wear reinforces your message. And if you are wearing a jacket and are being interviewed sitting down, tuck the tail of the jacket under your bottom to prevent it riding up and making you look like a hunchback on camera. If there is time, it is worth ringing to check the colours of the backdrop before you set off for the studio so that you don't find your clothes clash with it; black and grey work well with even the most violent background colours, but with a sombre backdrop women interviewees may look better in something bright. Traditionally, the background in every television news studio was blue and feature programmes were swathed in pastel shades; these days the BBC's news colour is orange.

You should always check your hair before the camera starts rolling; a stray wisp or two can drive viewers to distraction. If you are a woman going out on location to be interviewed, take a can of industrial strength hairspray with you: it may be a blowy day. Next you should look in the mirror again, carefully: I have known quite senior businessmen to do an entire interview with a pencil tucked behind their ear or an airline boarding pass protruding from their breast pocket. And if you're a conference delegate or have been given a visitor's pass to the studio, make sure you take your pass off. If you don't look tidy, your audience will wonder if your mind, your opinions or your business are equally disorganised. If you wear spectacles but you can manage without them or with contact lenses, you should check both options in the mirror; thick glasses reflect studio lighting in particular and create an impression of remoteness, but equally the heat from the lighting can dry up your contacts in a long programme.

At the very last minute you should go to the lavatory, even if you don't think you need to; it's amazing how your bladder can start to itch when you get on the air, and if it's a long, live programme there's no escape. Take any loose keys or coins out of your pocket that might jangle. Stub out your cigarette. And if you are carrying a mobile or a pager, switch it off: there's nothing worse when you're in full flight on television than your mobile ringing, and a surprising number of people caught like that actually try to answer.

Before you go on the air, you need above all to get your message straight. What is the basic point you want to get across? Make up a soundbite and memorise it, trying it on a friend if you have the opportunity. It shouldn't be long – American research suggests that if it's more than about eight seconds long, the audience won't remember it. The most effective soundbites are even shorter: remember Tony Blair's 'tough on crime and tough on the causes of crime'? The wordier it is, the less spontaneous it will sound as well; you don't want to end up like the policemen you see on television dramas reading suspects their rights. If you stick to simple words you also won't trip over them if you're a little nervous in front of the cameras. And if you're under fire, make sure your soundbite is positive and, above all, that it doesn't repeat the criticism. Write the soundbite down if necessary and keep looking at it before the interview starts, but don't forget: on television, you can't pick anything up and read it. People interviewed at home or in their office sometimes forget this, and fish out some document and try to read it out or brandish it in front of the camera. This looks disastrous on television; filming will be halted and you will be politely asked to put it away. The only exception is if you are publicising a book or a pamphlet; if you ask the producer or reporter for a chance to hold it up so the audience can see it, they may agree – though in my experience they often choose to forget.

It is in nobody's interests for you to go on the air unprepared. Before you are interviewed, you should give a little thought to obvious questions you may be asked and look up any facts you will find useful, or simple things that anyone in your position would look silly if they didn't know. You should assume that your interviewer will have little advance knowledge of complex technical issues, and the time to brief them is before the cameras start rolling – not in the limited time available for you to reach out to the viewers.

When you get to the studio

Be prepared to spend far longer in the television studios than it will take to broadcast or record your programme. Television isn't a simple medium, and you have to fit in with its way of doing things. Particularly if you are not being broadcast live, you will spend a lot of time waiting around even if your actual studio time is brief. So make allowance for this if you have children or pets at home, or other appointments in your diary. The last thing you need if you are going on television is to feel in a hurry.

If you are going to the studio, don't arrive with a fan club unless you have been asked to bring guests to sit in the audience. You need to have your mind on the job in hand, and as little as possible to distract you. It's quite justifiable if you are representing an organisation to take along a colleague to brief you and monitor the proceedings, providing they don't interfere or try to hog the limelight: they can check the set-up in the studio for you, time the various panellists' contributions if there are any concerns about political balance, and tell you how you came across. But otherwise you should go on your own. In particular you should not take young children with you and expect the studio staff to babysit them.

The first thing you need to ascertain when you get to the studio is who is in charge. Is it the reporter who is about to interview you, or is there a producer who is in control of the proceedings? Once you are sure, there are a few questions you should ask that person. First of all, double-check that the subject of the programme or interview is as previously discussed. This is important. Some television producers, including at least two of my acquaintance, have made their careers out of offering a guest a soft interview on subject A, then sandbagging them with subject B. So before you get into the studio, you need to get this straight.

Next you should confirm whether it is live or pre-recorded. Will it be repeated, and if so, when? If the programme is a discussion, is the journalist in the chair an inquisitor who will grill the interviewees, or a moderator who will simply ensure fair play? For how long will you be on the air? If the interview is being recorded for later use, how much of it is actually likely to be transmitted? And importantly, is the programme being shown only in your region or is it being networked to other parts of the country? I once accompanied a senior Scottish politician to a BBC programme being transmitted live from Edinburgh, only to discover as we left the studio that it was being shown everywhere except in Scotland.

If it is your first visit to the studio, you will need to get your bearings. If you get there early, the producer or a member of the production team may well show you to a hospitality suite well stocked with newspapers, a television monitor, coffee, Danish pastries – and probably booze. Whatever you do, and no matter how badly you feel like a drink, don't take any alcohol. Your pals may have told you it will help you relax, but after even a single drink your reactions become less sharp, your defences start to lower and you will have difficulty getting awkward words and phrases off your tongue. Just as important, after one drink you may very well feel like a second one if there's time, and very few people on television can carry off a large ingestion of alcohol like the late Reggie Bosanquet, who used to make it downstairs for a quick one at the nearest wine bar in the interval of *News at Ten*. Coffee is fine, though; a cup before the programme will keep you alert, particularly if you have had a hard day at work or are going on the air late at night. If you haven't eaten, don't feel shy about grabbing a sandwich: the amount of food left over from television hospitality suites would keep thousands from starvation. This is also a good moment to take your gum out if you have been chewing – or to put out that nerve-settling cigarette. Smoking on television these days is a no-no, not least because in the studio it may make your fellow contributors cough.

Before a discussion programme, you will quite often find your fellow panellists waiting in the hospitality suite. If an amicable chat is in prospect, it is quite handy to strike up a rapport beforehand. But if the rest of the panel are likely to give you a hard time on the programme, it is better not to arrive too early in case things start going downhill before you even get into the studio. Above all, be careful what you say beforehand to potentially hostile panellists – they may use it against you on the air.

Wherever the person in charge asks you to wait until they are ready for you, make sure you stay there – they'll come for you when they're ready. Television studios can be confusing places, with one corridor looking very like another, and if you wander off and the production team can't find you they will simply let the other items on the programme overrun and you will have lost your chance to put over your case. They may also hesitate before asking you back. If you get really lost, you could even stumble into a studio where another programme is being made, with all sorts of disastrous consequences.

You should also keep out of the way of people trying to make programmes. If the team producing yours has time for a chat, fine – it will put you at ease. You may also get a chance to meet the presenter of the programme and strike up a rapport, and he or she may well give you an outline of the kind of questions they are going to ask – and even of what they would like you to say. Yet you should try, in your nervousness, to avoid badgering studio staff if they are obviously trying to put together a programme against a deadline.

Before you go into the studio, you may be asked if you would like to go into make-up. If this offer is made, accept it – it isn't an insult. Professional television make-up artists are expert at both putting participants in programmes at their ease and, with a comb and a brush or two of face powder, making you look that little bit fresher and better groomed than when you walked into the building. Even if you have shaved or done your own make-up just before you left home, there are ways of improving your colouring or facial texture before you go on the air – and the better you look, the more what you say will be listened to. Always remember, Richard Nixon refused make-up before his crucial television debate with John F. Kennedy in 1960 and his decision probably cost him the Presidency: his five o'clock shadow gave him a haunted, untrustworthy look.

Just one reminder if you are given studio make-up: once the programme is over, remember to ask for a tissue so you can wipe it off, and look in a mirror before you go home or back to your job. Sometimes even a light application of powder to make you look better under the television lights will make you appear really odd in daylight or under conventional lighting.

Usually a production assistant will escort you into the studio when your time to go on the air or be recorded is approaching. If the programme is live or filming is already under way, you will be asked before you go in to be quiet and stand still and out of the way, and to wait until a particular moment to take your seat or your place behind the desk. Do what they tell you. Even if the programme is live they will be able to move you in without the viewers noticing, provided you keep quiet and make sure you don't trip over any of the cables criss-crossing the studio floor. Studio silence can be broken while pre-recorded packages are shown and during commercial breaks, and you may even be shown to your place when the cameras have panned to the weather girl, sports reporter or financial analyst at the other end of the studio. Before you go on the air you will be told whether to look into a particular camera or towards the presenter; while you are getting these final instructions a member of the crew will be 'miking you up' – pinning a little microphone to your clothing within, say, nine inches of your mouth and, if necessary, feeding the wire inside your jacket or up your sleeve to make it inconspicuous. If they ask you to undo your shirt or untuck your blouse, co-operate – don't slap them. Shortly before the programme or the interview begins, you will probably be asked to say a few words as a 'sound check' to make sure that the system is working and your voice is at the right volume. Whether you are miked up or not, you should only speak if you are spoken to in case you are on the air or your comments are being fed out of the studio.

If you are in a busy studio with a presenter and maybe some other panellists plus a production team and maybe a studio audience, you are lucky; you know where you stand. My own pet hate – though it was not hard to master – is the 'remote', a small studio in which the interviewee or contributor speaks direct to a camera remotely controlled from another studio, responding to questions or prompting from an unseen interviewer or producer miles away. If you are in the regions and being interviewed for a national programme you may very well find yourself in a 'remote'; most interviews for BBC breakfast television are done this way. There is even a 'remote' in Broadcasting House, the London head-quarters of the BBC, where you can be interviewed for local news programmes.

Remotes vary: there may or may not be a production assistant to supervise the interview. You may have the soundtrack from the programme played to you over a loudspeaker, or be given an incon-spicuous earpiece to listen to it. And don't be surprised if there's a plain coloured cloth behind you – by a miracle of back-projection technology you will appear on the screen with Big Ben, your own city centre or some other appropriate scene in shot.

As with all other appearances on television, you need to keep your nerve if you are in a remote. You must keep paying attention to the programme being fed to you, so that you don't miss your cue or find yourself being asked to respond to a comment you weren't listening to. And although there's a monitor there to show you how you look on television, you must ignore it after an initial glance to double-check that you look all right; if you stare at it while you are meant to be looking at the camera, you will come over as shifty in the extreme.

There is one other piece of television technology that novices find unnerving: the teleprompter or autocue. It isn't often that non-professional contributors are asked to use one, but if you have been asked to prepare a statement beforehand for delivery and it is too long to memorise, you may find yourself having to read it off one of these machines. Even if you have read through your script before-hand and are comfortable with it, it is unnerving to find yourself live on television, looking at the camera with the words you are to speak being scrolled up a screen just above it. The one thing you must avoid doing – and I always found this difficult when I reviewed the papers for the *Channel Four Daily* – is falling into the trap of racing the autocue. The person operating it will scroll up your words as you speak them, and will keep going at your pace. If you slow down, they will slow down, but it's a natural instinct to think that the words are slipping away and you must try to keep up – in which case the operator will go faster and faster to keep up with you. Some autocues you can operate yourself with a pedal; the risk with these is that your foot can slip and the entire script will whizz past you in seconds, leaving you stranded.

On location

If the television crew is coming to your home or office to interview you, or meeting you on location, there are quite a few things you need to bear in mind. To begin with: is there room? In the 1970s a busload of technical staff on generous union rates would accompany any reporter and home interviews were impracticable; now just a reporter and cameraman are likely to turn up, and on some cash-strapped cable stations the reporter will even do their own filming. Even so, they will need to be able to mount their camera far enough away from you to get a decent shot, and many living rooms are simply too small for this. If they also have to bring either their own lighting or one of those white discs or umbrellas which amplify the lighting already available, that will take up space as well. And if you have a soundman waving a boom mike on a pole ('one of those furry things', as the first President Bush, a frequent victim, called them), watch out for your china ornaments.

You need to do the interview where you feel most comfortable and relaxed. If there's a room or a sofa you feel particularly happy with, suggest it to the television crew. And if there simply isn't anywhere indoors where you feel comfortable and the light is good enough, there may be an agreeable spot in the garden. Check the background. Shelves full of books add gravity to what you are saying, a giant portrait of Pamela Anderson won't. A view through the French windows to the countryside beyond adds an impression of tranquillity. You need to put the crew at their ease too – a cup of tea will work wonders, but there's no need to lay on a three-course meal.

Recording your television interview shouldn't be a free show for your neighbours and relatives; you will find it easier to be yourself if the house isn't full of people trying to see how a programme is made or straining to get into the picture. If you are representing an organisation it will, however, be handy to have a colleague along to rehearse key points with you, even if they don't appear on air. The interviewer may want to get your spouse or partner in shot, and maybe your children or even your pets if they will add to the impact or appeal of the story. Otherwise you should get a neighbour to look after your children so they don't stray into shot or start scrapping in mid-interview, and tell other members of the family, on pain of death, not to start hoovering or switch on the radio. Unplug the telephone, too, and try to eliminate any background noise.

If the crew come to see you at work or at the premises of the organisation you represent, you should seek out a spacious, uncluttered room so that they can set up and interview you. You can organise a backdrop featuring the name of your business (you never see a football manager or racing driver interviewed these days without their sponsor's logo behind them), or a poster giving the name of your campaign organisation or saying what you are fighting for. Anything like this helps to establish who you are with the viewers before you have even opened your mouth, and leaves them with a strong visual message. But make sure the letters and the images are bold and simple – acres of small print behind you will just be a distraction. Make certain, too, that it is securely fastened and won't fall down during the interview.

As I mentioned earlier, if your organisation is doing something with people – a pensioners' exercise class or a day nursery, maybe – make sure at the very least that the camera crew get a shot of them, and at best that the interview is filmed with the activity going on in the background. Similarly, if you are promoting your business and can get whatever your firm does into shot, you will leave the viewer with strong positive images.

If you are interviewed out in the open, be careful to choose the right spot. The reporter and crew, as professionals, will pick out the location that is right for them, but you need to make sure it is right for you. Are you adequately screened from other people straying into shot and waving at the camera, or people who don't share your views turning the event to your disadvantage? Are there animals around, even dogs being walked, that could disrupt the proceedings? I have seen a live interview outside the House of Commons come close to disaster when a dog on an extending lead slunk across the green behind the interviewee and cocked its leg against his. Luckily its owner pulled the dog away in the nick of time, without the MP ever knowing how close he had come to a lost deposit.

You need to find somewhere quiet: passing trains, chainsaws, ice-cream van chimes and church clocks can all madden television crews with limited time to get an interview into the can, and each time you do a retake both you and the interviewer stand a greater chance of making a fluff. Make sure you don't stand in front of something that would distract the viewer, make you look silly or even undermine your case. If you're campaigning in an election, for instance, don't stand underneath one of your opponent's posters – you would be better off not appearing at all. Keep well away from other people's bonfires; with a change of wind, the smoke will not only ruin the picture but you may find it hard to talk without coughing. And above all, don't stand just in front of, say, a sandpit, a pond, a low wall or a sheer drop. It's all too easy to take a step or two back during the interview and end up base over apex; quite apart from the embarrassment, there may not be time for you to go home for a bath and a change of clothes and then shoot the interview again. Nor are you doing the interview so that you can show up years later on *It'll Be Alright on the Night*.

Conversely, you should also make sure that the television crew don't wreck the proceedings. Cameramen can be heavy-footed and if they step backwards while filming, in particular, accidents can happen. There are classic instances of them knocking over a chain of dominoes being constructed for the *Guinness Book of Records*, stepping on the eggs of the sole nesting bird of a particular species in Britain which they have travelled miles to film – and even, as happened in Shetland after the wreck of the oil tanker *Braer*, running over the endangered animal who was the reason for their visit. So if there is anything precious or delicate on the ground, make extra sure the camera crew know just where it is, warn them to be careful, and get someone you can trust to stay with them.

Just before they start to film, put down your handbag or take out of your pocket any keys or coins that you might feel tempted to jangle while you are being filmed: mannerisms like this look very bad on television. And ask a friend if you look OK – you still have time to adjust your tie or your hair, or even move something unsightly out of the background, as long as you are quick about it.

The cameraman or crew won't only film you as you are being interviewed. Once the interview is finished, they will probably want to film a quick 'cutaway' shot showing you and the interviewer in conversation. During this bit of filming it doesn't matter what you talk about as the soundtrack won't be recording; nevertheless you should say nothing you might be embarrassed about, as there have been instances of people who can lip-read picking up stray remarks uttered during a cutaway shot and taking umbrage. You may also be asked for a 'walking shot', approaching and then passing the camera; you often see these on news bulletins to introduce someone just before they are interviewed. In my view they make rotten television, but no one seems to have thought of anything better.

One form of interview on location offers great hazards because it is totally unexpected: the 'ambush' on a controversial subject that you are either unaware of until that moment or would prefer to avoid. How many times have you seen some politician, business leader or shady character surprised by a television reporter who has simply turned up with a mike and a camera to ask awkward or immediate questions? If you are in a position of responsibility, it could very well happen to you, and if it does, your immediate reactions determine whether you come out on top.

For a start, you have very little choice over whether to speak. If you simply tell the reporter (or pack of reporters) 'I have nothing to say' and move off, they will get film of you avoiding the question, and you need to have an exceptionally good reason to do this. If you run off or take a swing at one of them, that will look even worse. If the subject takes you completely by surprise, you can say: 'I will have to look into this and will give you a comment just as soon as I can.' And if the matter sounds a serious one, for goodness' sake don't make light of it – the contrast with the rest of the news package broadcast by the station will leave you looking heartless.

With a TV ambush, your body language is crucial. For a start, if you are carrying a briefcase, put it down. Media trainers find that, time after time, the victims of ambushes hang on to their briefcase as a kind of comfort blanket, and that during the interview it turns into a useless appendage that hampers their movement. Once the questioning has begun, it's hard to put your briefcase down, so do it straight away. You also need to face the cameras four-square for as long as you are speaking; if you look throughout the questioning as though you are desperate to slip away, you will come across as having something to hide. This doesn't mean that you have to cede control; you should take what you consider a reasonable number of questions and then bring the interview politely to a close. Equally, if you have a number of reporters interrupting each other, you should answer whichever of their questions suits you best. Sometimes on a controversial story you will also have members of the public interrupting; with them you should be polite, but firm. If there is a group of people concerned about whatever you are doing, you should offer to meet them separately but in private. Sometimes such groups have been organised or fired up by the media and there is no reason why you should give currency to a campaign aimed against you.

On the air

The camera has started to roll and the interviewer is about to put the first question to you. You have glanced briefly in the monitor to make sure you have got your tie straight or your hair in place, and are now facing the interviewer (or the remote camera), as requested. You have butterflies in your stomach, your mouth suddenly feels dry and a huge audience is about to see you and hear what you have to say. You're on your own now, so how do you handle it?

The most important thing to remember is to *be yourself.* Try to be as natural as possible; you will forget the moment the interview gets under way that there are millions of people watching out there. So be sincere and look convincing; if you don't look as if you believe what you are saying, nobody out there is going to believe you. You should be positive if you are under pressure, though if the subject is a serious or delicate one it is a mistake to look too bullish. Equally, you should take care never to look defensive or shifty; it is particularly important to maintain eye contact with the interviewer.

When your turn comes to talk, *speak firmly, yet conversationally.* Remember: you are speaking to people in their homes, not to a

Nuremberg rally. Be spontaneous; nothing turns off an audience more thoroughly than a robotic delivery. Try not to speak too fast, and also not too loud. Try also to *avoid irritating mannerisms* like clutching your chin, tugging your ears, fiddling with your tie or rubbing your hands together. With television, your body language matters almost as much as what you say; if you look nervous, people will wonder if you are on top of your subject – and maybe whether you are telling the truth. You mustn't freeze on screen so that you look like an android, but you should remember that television exaggerates the smallest gesture. If you are interviewed out of doors and standing up, you can and should be expressive with your hands. But particularly if you are sitting behind a desk, overusing your arms and hands, and excessive facial contortions, will make you look hyperactive. Everyone of a certain age remembers the expressive Dr Magnus Pyke with his flailing arms – but does anyone remember what he had to say?

As the interview goes on, even if it's a brief one of two or three minutes, you can develop a relationship with the interviewer (and with the other panellists if it's a discussion). Listen carefully to the questions; if you aren't clear what the interviewer means, ask them to clarify. And *answer the questions one at a time*; if you are asked several at once, choose the one you feel happiest about answering. Only avoid answering a specific question if you can turn it round by offering a relevant, positive fact. And try to avoid one-word answers unless you can follow them up with a longer explanation; otherwise you will wrong-foot the interviewer and trigger an awkward pause.

Above all, you must *concentrate*. It's easy to drift off when the discussion switches to another participant or to the other end of the studio. But you should never forget when someone else is speaking that the camera may suddenly come back to you. So don't slump in your seat or start inspecting your nails. And keep listening to what is being said in case you are suddenly called on to speak.

As early as you can in the interview, you need to *flag up your soundbite* with a phrase like 'Of course the really important thing to remember is ...' and then use it. Back it up with any supporting facts – and if you get a chance, use it again later in the interview. If you are on live, this will underline your message; if the programme is being recorded it lessens the chance that the point you particularly want to make will be cut out.

You should *stick to the point*, unless the interviewer has been giving you a hard time and inadvertently offers you the opportunity to ease the pressure by changing the subject. But you don't want to veer so far off course that they can seize back the high ground by saying that you're trying to evade the question. Nevertheless, if the interviewer goes off at a tangent and then takes you to task for raising irrelevances, it's perfectly in order to say: 'But that was the question you asked.' And if the interviewer does wander, make extra sure that you manage to get in your soundbite. If necessary, just come out with it even if it has nothing to do with the question. After all, you were invited on the programme to get your point across.

Don't be afraid to correct the interviewer; you need not do it in a hostile way. If the question put to you is based on a false assumption or misrepresents your case, you should point it out politely and then give the facts as you understand them. But if the error is a small one or isn't strictly relevant to the points you want to raise, dismiss it as briefly as possible and then press on with what you went on the air to say. You occasionally see interviews in which a participant trying to correct a small point loses the big picture and ends up wasting their opportunity.

If the interviewer – or another panellist – says anything you strongly disagree with, *you are free to interrupt*. It can make good television, but you should be sparing when you do it. Equally, don't be surprised if someone does it to you. If someone persists in inter-rupting you, you can say firmly to them: 'Just let me finish answering your original question.' If they become boorish and keep overstepping the mark, the interviewer will generally deal with them – you shouldn't need to take on that role yourself.

If a negative question is put to you, *turn it round into a positive*. This is a golden opportunity to take control. Suppose the interviewer says: 'Isn't it the case that your restructuring programme will inflict hardship on the community by putting 150 skilled craftsmen out of work?' Don't agree – come back with something upbeat if you can, like: 'Far from it. We have offered jobs in our other plant to sixty of our most highly skilled workers, and all the others will be offered retraining. The future of all our workforce matters to us, and we will do everything possible to make sure that as many as possible move on to high-quality jobs even if we cannot provide them all ourselves. That way, the future of the community will be assured.' Don't, as one of my media trainees did when pressed on the kind of retraining skilled manual workers would receive, volunteer 'flower arranging' as the answer – the responses you give in a broadcast interview must above all be appropriate.

Humour can be a valuable and effective weapon, but you must avoid being flippant or tasteless; if you are trying to make a serious point, excessive levity will at best detract from your message and at worst make you look gauche and uncaring. Remember how, the day after the *Herald of Free Enterprise* disaster, the late Nicholas Ridley praised a colleague in the House of Commons for 'navigating with his bow doors closed'. . . and how his remarks were received.

Now some other important don'ts:

- *Don't confuse the viewers by raising too many issues*. Make a few points (maybe only one) and make them clearly.
- *Don't raise fresh, extraneous issues* that draw attention away from the case you are trying to make. You may think being on television is a golden opportunity to publicise some other cause you are

promoting, but you will almost certainly do yourself more harm than good. If the programme is recorded, your comments will almost certainly be edited out. Or worse still, the extraneous material will be kept in and your main point won't be covered.

- *Don't volunteer bad news.* If you are the manager of plant A which is facing possible closure, don't reveal to the interviewer and your audience that plant B, which nobody had realised to be at risk, is also under threat. You are on the programme to improve your image or limit the damage, not to dig a bigger hole for yourself. But you would be surprised how many people do it.

- *Don't say: 'No comment'.* It's an admission of guilt or liability. If you didn't want to comment, you shouldn't have come on the programme.

- *Don't waffle.* Say what you have to say, then stop. If the programme is being recorded and you realise you have lost the thread of what you are saying, you can ask for a retake. Very occasionally the tape with the 'fluff' on it mistakenly gets into the final programme instead of the retake, particularly if it has been put together in a great hurry. So never take the risk some daring broadcasters take, and slip in an obscenity once they know the tape won't go out: the night Brent Sadler was seen saying 'Oh, shit!' on *News at Ten* after mispronouncing a Russian diplomat's name in a pre-recorded package, ITN's switchboard was jammed with complainers, and Sadler's argument that he thought the tape wasn't going to be used as he had redone his words to camera correctly did not impress the management.

- *Don't use jargon or acronyms.* You can't expect people to relate to you if you tie yourself up in technicalities and use words or initials they don't understand.

- *Don't blind your audience with statistics.* Used sparingly they can be powerful support for your case, but reel them off to excess and you will sound like a nerd. And if you sidestep the issue by spouting statistics, viewers may well conclude that your argument doesn't stand up.

- *Don't lose your cool.* It may be difficult to stay calm if the interviewer or a fellow panellist gets confrontational, but if you can resist the temptation to get back at them, you will have captured the high ground. Lose your cool, and you will lose your audience. The former Conservative Defence Secretary John Nott is still remembered for storming out of a major interview with Robin Day, two decades after it happened.
- *Don't get overconfident.* If you start thinking an interview's a doddle, and particularly if you stop listening carefully to what the other people are saying, you can trip up badly. Always remember: the next question may be a stinker.
- *Don't smile if the news is bad.* Nothing will do more harm to the case you are trying to put across than if you accompany some serious remark with a huge cheesy grin.
- *Don't guess.* If you haven't got a fact ready in your head, it's tempting to busk it. But someone out there will know the real answer. Instead you should offer up another fact that is relevant. If the interviewer persists, tell him you will make sure the programme gets the facts as soon as they are available.
- *Don't patronise your audience or fellow panellists.* If you come across as self-opinionated, smug, ingratiating or arrogant compared with them, you are shooting yourself in the foot.
- *Don't yawn.* If you look or sound bored, why should anyone watching the programme be interested in what you have to say? Worse still, don't fall asleep. Television studios are pretty airless places and the studio lighting can be hot, so you need to stay alert. If you feel yourself going, breathe deeply and then take a sip of water. And if you do nod off, just pray you don't snore!

- *Don't swear.* Some people lapse into coarse language almost without thinking, and except possibly on a lads' chat show it will always mark you down. It may also lead some people to think you have been drinking. And it may very well guarantee that you never appear on that particular programme or station again. There is no point that cannot be made forcibly in the English lanuguage without recourse to profanity. And remember, viewers generally are far more affronted by swearing on television than they are by sex or violence.

- *Don't make extravagant claims you can't substantiate.* Remember that someone out there may know the real situation – and may go to the media with it if you distort the facts, giving rise to further adverse publicity. Remember, also, the laws of libel – they apply to television every bit as much as to newspapers. It's easy when a television discussion really gets going to forget that anyone out there is watching, and to say what you really think of Mr X or repeat that little item of gossip you heard about Mrs Y. But it could cost you a packet in legal fees and libel damages.

- Finally, *don't lie.* You are bound to be caught out.

Winding up

You can usually tell when the programme is drawing to a close. The floor manager will start gesticulating at the interviewer. There may be a clock ticking round to the time you are due to come off the air. The presenter may even turn to the panel and ask for quick answers.

If you have just a short time to go, don't breathe a sigh of relief: there is an opportunity to be taken, for you know you have that much time to get your key argument across once again. Lord Thorneycroft, an accomplished and ruthless politician in the early days of broadcasting, used to advise colleagues: 'The moment you know the programme is going to end, start talking no matter what is going on in the studio and keep going till the cameras stop.' I saw him do it a couple of times, and it was highly effective; I imagine the other participants gave him a rough time afterwards, but by then it was too late.

You don't have to be as confrontational as that. But the moment you can see the programme is drawing to a close, you should take whatever opportunity you can to use that soundbite of yours one last time. And in a panel discussion, you should do your level best to speak last – that way you leave a lasting impression with the audience. You also make quite sure that no one else can come in after you with some killer comment that undoes all your good work during the programme. But if you do start talking and the cameras resolutely stay fixed on another guest, pipe down – if you continue, all the viewers will hear is someone interrupting the person they can see talking, and that won't do you any good.

At the end of any live programme, and usually at the end of any interview done in the studio, the interviewer or presenter will wind up with a 'Thank you very much' or a 'Goodnight' to the audience. The music and closing credits will roll, and the cameras will be switched off. You can then have your mike taken off and are free to go. Don't say anything until you are sure it won't be broadcast or recorded occasionally the sound system is inadvertently left switched on and some disembodied remark is broadcast into people's homes.

If you are only on for a segment of a programme, you may well be ushered out of the studio as soon as you have finished and with the programme still in full swing. Don't move from your seat until your mike has been taken off or you may go sprawling. As on arrival, you should keep as quiet as possible as you move through the studio, and watch out for cables and other obstacles you might trip over.

When you get to the big studio door, open and shut it gently if the cameras are still rolling.

After the interview, there may well be a chance to wind down: at home with the reporter over a cup of tea, or at the studios over a drink with the production team and any other panellists. This is a useful opportunity to prepare the ground for a follow-up or to establish contact with people who may be useful to you. But it is also a time when all the good work done during the programme can be spoiled by an unguarded word now the pressure is off. Be careful, in particular, not to down a couple of drinks and then get candid – or, worse still, pick a fight. The impression you leave in the television studio is at least as important to your case as the one you make on the screen.

Before you step out into the street, you should look in the mirror one last time – and make quite sure there are no traces left of television make-up. Make sure also that you haven't left any belongings behind.

If you have been interviewed on some issue of major or even local importance, don't be surprised if local radio or the papers either report what you said or ring you wanting to know more. If you want the publicity, give them all the help you can and bear them in mind as the story develops.

Whatever the nature of your interview, don't be too surprised if it is repeated months or even years later. Feature programmes are quite often repeated, and even news clips can turn up much later in unexpected situations. It took me some time to recover from seeing a current affairs interview I had done for Central Television crop up months later as 'wallpaper' in an episode of the thriller series *Boon*.

4   Sounding your best on radio

Radio is the most effective medium of all for communication. Through it, you can get your point across to other people with the minimum of distractions; indeed, the best broadcasters use the microphone not to address a mass audience, but to speak to each person listening as if they were in conversation with a friend. Consider Alistair Cooke's legendary *Letter from America*: it sounds like an unscripted fifteen-minute ramble, but not a word is wasted and the listener gets up from their chair with a vivid word picture in their mind. It is far harder to achieve such total communication through television, as by and large the picture gets in the way. And while a well-written newspaper article can make a real impact, more concentration is needed from the reader than is required of the listener.

The classic example of the differing impacts of the two electronic media is that first Kennedy–Nixon debate in 1960. Television viewers voted Kennedy the winner because Nixon looked haggard and strained; but the radio audience, still massive in those days but less glamorous for the media, put Nixon ahead because they felt he had the better arguments. On radio, substance wins over style every time, provided you have a warm, interesting, authoritative manner of delivery.

So if you have a case to put across or an argument to refute, radio is the medium for you – and all the more so if you are not a professional communicator. You don't need to worry about whether people watching at home will like your tie or whether your hairdo is coming adrift; all they will get from you is your words and, hopefully, your sincerity. Yet the very features that make radio such an effective medium also make it important that you treat the microphone and the audience beyond it with respect, so that you maximise the opportunity you have been handed to communicate. There is a narrow divide between being relaxed in front of the mike, which will create a closeness with your listeners, and being over-casual, which loses them.

The vastly simpler process of producing a radio programme means that it is both a more informal and a more intimate medium than television. A radio reporter coming to see you will have just a mike and a tape or mini disc recorder; contrast that with the camera, tripod, furry mike and lights or reflective disc that even the smallest television crew will bring. Studios for even the most prestigious radio programmes, like Radio 4's *Today*, usually contain only a simple table with microphones, with a studio manager behind a glass panel operating the tape machine; no teams of technicians, no cameras and autocue machines, no snazzy set or colourful backdrop. Indeed, the overwhelming impression in any radio studio is of frugality. Yet from these basic surroundings comes the most compulsive listening, and often the biggest news. Indeed, *Today* sets the agenda for the entire BBC and much of the rest of the media: most politicians listen to it, and the competition to bag the 8.10am slot after the news is intense.

The phone-in

For most people with something to get off their chest or an event or cause to publicise, the local radio phone-in is the perfect vehicle. A few high-profile presenters use the phone-in as an opportunity to shock or to ridicule the participants, but most such programmes provide an unrivalled opportunity for the man or woman in the street to communicate with a wide and receptive audience. The phone-in is assumed by many, not without reason at times, to be a forum for the opinionated and the ill-informed, but anyone who gets onto such a programme and talks sense will be surprised by the impact they make.

For this reason, political parties and other large commercial or campaigning organisations find it worth their while to get supportive voices on to such programmes; if there is a debate in progress about, say, the need to improve the health service, the mood of the listeners can be swayed by an apparently independent citizen giving a strong example of excellent or abysmal patient care. So if you know a phone-in is about to be broadcast which has a bearing on your own company or organisation, it's well worth lining up a few callers to support your case. However, you need to be careful of three things. First, that they aren't so overenthusiastic or so numerous that it is evident to the radio station that you are trying to pack the programme. Second, that you don't put up people who would have to admit, if pressed, that they are on your payroll: that would get into the papers, and leave you looking devious or worse. And third, that you can trust them to say what you want them to say.

Before you take part in a phone-in, you need to be clear in your mind what message you want to get across. Your message needs to be simple and uncluttered, so it's worth writing down the points you want to make before you pick up the phone. Limit yourself to a single topic, have a simple soundbite and two or three details or supporting facts ready – and it's tactful to make a note of the presenter's name. There's nothing more embarrassing than forgetting, or worse still, getting it wrong.

If you are listening to a phone-in and some comment enrages you, count to ten before picking up the phone. And if you have had a few drinks, put the temptation right out of your mind – your clever idea after a few pints may sound pretty crass on the air. As with any other contact with the media, you also need quickly to ask yourself if a comment from you might make the situation worse for yourself, or open up some further argument that could cause you damage. Only if you are sure there are no minuses should you make that call. And if you ring specifically to take issue with someone, it is more important than ever to be able to back up your argument with hard facts.

Every radio station has a different procedure for taking listeners' calls for a phone-in, and there is no guarantee that you will get on the air (for this reason you should never count on publicising anything through a phone-in alone). Some (notably national) stations like you to ring in beforehand so that they can call you back once they know how the points you want to make would fit into the discussion. Others expect you to ring during the programme, and may put you in a queue. The smaller stations may stick you straight on the air, so make sure you're ready to speak – and rehearse what you want to say first, in case there are any awkward words you will trip over. If there are, you need to find simpler ones. Don't forget to switch your own radio off before you pick up the phone, as the feedback from it will interfere with your own call, and it's best to shut your door and switch off your mobile. Shut up any animals too – there's nothing worse than having a cat jump on you when you're in mid-sentence, as happened to me once.

Once you're through to the station, keep silent unless you are being spoken to; otherwise you may say something on the air without realising you have an audience. The station may well pipe the programme down the line to you before it's your turn to speak so that you can hear the previous discussion; if they don't volunteer to, ask if they would mind doing it. The conversation will usually open with some small talk, and then you will be asked why you are ringing. You need to get straight to the point as you don't know how much time you will get. Even if your argument is really persuasive, you may find yourself with just thirty seconds before a news bulletin or a commercial break, and there is no guarantee the presenter will come back to you. So make your point or your announcement, get in your soundbite and put across whatever facts are important to you. But remember to be conversational and sound spontaneous; there's nothing worse than hearing a caller on a phone-in painstakingly read out some carefully drafted statement. You should also remember to speak slowly; it's easy to get nervous and gabble, and if you do, your words will lose their impact. And above all, don't rant: to get your point across to the listening audience, you have to appear sane and rational.

Of course, the phone-in isn't a one-way medium. You should expect the presenter to ask you some questions, and you should be ready for the more obvious ones. There may be other callers on the line; you will have the chance to react to their points of view, and they to yours. You should always extend to them the tolerance you would expect in any conversation; they are entitled to their views and it is the function of the presenter to open up a discussion. So even if you passionately disagree with what another participant is saying, stay calm, reasonable and polite. Otherwise you will end up losing the sympathy of your audience and maybe even having the plug pulled on you. If another caller is aggressive towards you, try to rise above it. The presenter should slap down really boorish participants, and if he or she doesn't, you should stick up for yourself without losing your temper, for example by telling them politely but firmly not to interrupt and to listen to what you have to say just as you listened to them. Don't forget, also, that the laws of libel apply to radio just as much as to television and newspapers. And if you rubbish someone who isn't on the programme, there's always the chance that they may be listening at home or in their car; they may even ring in and get their own back.

If the presenter gives you enough time, it is well worth returning to the point you wanted to make – and of course repeating your soundbite. If you are publicising an event, repeat where and when it is being held. If you repeat your key message, the audience stand a much better chance of remembering what you went on the radio to say once your call has ended or they have switched off.

Once the presenter decides you have had your say, he or she will say goodbye to you or simply switch to another caller. The producer may come on and thank you, but you are just as likely simply to hear the dialling tone. Strange things can happen with the wiring in radio studios, so it is safer once again not to say anything that might escape onto the air before you hang up.

Preparing for a radio interview

The ground rules for a radio interview of any kind are almost the same as for television, so you have the same questions to ask yourself. Why do they want to interview you? Is it wise for you to appear? Is there someone else who might put the case better? Are you going on to tell the audience something or to be grilled? Who will the programme be aimed at? Are you going on live or is the programme recorded? Is there anyone else being interviewed who might gang up on you? What will the first question be, and if there is more than one interviewee who will answer it first?

But there are extra questions you should ask that are specific to radio. For a start, many radio interviews at a distance are done 'down the line' by telephone rather than by the reporter calling at your home – and sometimes the reporter will already be broadcasting when they come to you. So you need at the very outset to ascertain whether you are live. Nor – unless, obviously, the programme is already on the air – do you usually have to do the interview straight away; unless time is pressing, you can generally ask if they will call back once you have got your facts together. It may also be worth your offering to fax or e-mail to the interviewer some of the facts behind the story, so that the questions will be better informed and will allow you to get your points across more effectively.

You should also make sure that the person on the line is in fact who they say they are – and if you have any doubts, you should take their number and call them back. The world of radio is full of jokesters: Sven-Goran Eriksson has been tricked several times by radio reporters claiming to be top football managers, and the Queen once had a long conversation on the air with a Montreal DJ who had got through the Buckingham Palace switchboard by pretending to be the Canadian Prime Minister. If you're not careful about who you take calls from, you could be next.

Producers of prestige programmes like *Today* always prefer to use interviews of studio quality. So if you can't get to the studio for any reason, they may offer to send a radio car which can do the interview from outside your home, rather than over the phone. The radio car – often a converted taxi – is in effect a studio on wheels: you sit in the back and speak into a static mike or a handset, which transmits your voice over a high-quality connection to the studio. All you have to do is wait for the car to arrive, check with the driver what you are supposed to do, get into the back and make contact with the studio. From your end, it's just like a telephone interview. Just one word of warning: unless the producer wants any of your neighbours to broadcast with you, don't let anyone else get in. Sometimes radio programmes want to interview you when you can't find anyone else to look after the children, but studio technicians can sense if you have taken them into the radio car with you, no matter how quiet and well behaved they are.

You can be saved all this palaver if you happen to have an ISDN telephone line – as installed by an increasing number of home computer users. ISDN gives studio quality, so if you have one and a radio station wants to interview you, there is the option of broadcasting from home instead of heading for the studio. If you live in the country the saving in travel time and general upheaval can be considerable. But remember, a studio-quality line will amplify all the other sounds in your home, so it is more important than ever that you suppress your family and animals and switch off all your machinery and other phones.

One joy of radio is that you are free to concentrate solely on what you intend to say and how you want to say it. Your appearance and body language won't matter, unless you look so strange that other people in the studio feel moved to comment. Nor do you have to rely on memory while making your contribution to the programme; you can write down the main points you want to make beforehand on a card (not paper – it rustles). If you are interviewed at home you can have it alongside you together with any other back-up material you may need, and if you are going to the studio you can take it along with you. People listening will never know you have a crib sheet, and the interviewer won't mind unless you start reciting from it in a deadpan fashion. During the programme you can also jot down points you want to make in response to other speakers, provided you don't make rustling noises; so take a pen with you – but not the type you have to click before you use it. One other hint on noise – the rattling of clunky jewellery, and especially bangles, sounds terrible on the air, so please take it off beforehand.

In the valuable time before the interview, the same considerations apply as with television. Work out what you want to say, and find a way of keeping it simple. Have your soundbite ready, and rehearse it. Think of any awkward questions you may be asked and have answers ready. And if you are in doubt about the pronunciation of any names, take the opportunity to check – if you get them wrong, your audience will wonder what else you don't know.

If you're nervous, make yourself a cup of tea. Avoid the temptation to have a stiff drink – after it you are never as firmly in control as you think you are, and the producer can spot the signs, even if not everyone in the audience can. Moreover, one drink can lead to another, and it is no coincidence that the most notorious radio broadcast of all time was Commander Tommy Woodruff's BBC report of the Spithead Review celebrating George V's Silver Jubilee, made after he had been regally entertained in the wardroom of his old ship. Woodruff's phrase 'the fleet's lit up' passed into the English language. Lord Deedes, who shared in the moment and the hospitality as a reporter for the *Morning Post*, told me: 'We thought Woodruff had just about got away with it. But when we got back to London we realised he hadn't.' So don't touch a drop.

If the interviewer is coming to see you, the recording will involve a minimum of disruption to your home or your routine. Unless the reporter is looking for sound effects like aircraft noise, cows mooing or the like, it doesn't matter where on your premises you do the interview, provided you are comfortable and free from interruptions. But it usually works best for sound quality if you both sit up at the kitchen table with the recorder between you, so that each voice is heard clearly. Before you start, make sure the phone is unplugged, your mobile is switched off and that children and animals are out of earshot. Don't have any adults in with you, unless the interviewer has said they would welcome a second voice. And don't encourage friends or neighbours to join you – they may hog the interview or come out with some opinion you disagree with.

If you have been invited into the studio and are faced with an awkward journey, the radio station – unless it is a very small one – will arrange a taxi for you. Make sure you are ready for when it arrives, and that you have the taxi firm's number in case it doesn't. It is usually best to go to the studio on your own, but if you are taking part in a high-profile discussion it may be handy to take along a colleague with whom you can rehearse the arguments. They can wait outside the studio while you are doing the programme and listen to the 'feed' to let you know how you have done.

There is just one thing you would be wise to take with you or pick up on the way: a bottle of water. Simply sitting in front of a mike makes many people's throats dry out, and you'll be surprised how much just a swig of water eases the situation. The BBC will often have a jug of water handy in the studio, but it's a sensible precaution to take your own.

Radio studios, as I've said, can be pretty basic places – and with the occasional exception the BBC's are the most spartan of all. You certainly won't find a lavish hospitality suite, but you may still be ushered into a small room with a jug of coffee to wait your turn. As with television, you can find yourself thrown together with fellow panellists who will give you a hard time on the air – if there is a risk of this, don't get there too early. In a large studio complex someone will come and fetch you from reception to make sure you don't get lost en route; in a smaller, local station you will simply wait in the front office and go through to a back room to do the broadcast. Don't be misled by the surroundings, however; good radio involves a high degree of professionalism, both in terms of the technology and the flow of the programme.

You may get a chance to talk over the shape of the programme and your contribution to it with the presenter/interviewer and any other participants before you go through to the studio. There is a last opportunity to check the subject of the interview and likely lines of questioning, and then it will be time to go through. Before you do, remember to go to the lavatory (a full bladder is a great distraction), take your chewing gum out (even more important with radio than with television) and switch off your mobile and your pager if you carry one. If you're smoking, put out your cigarette before you go into the studio, and don't be tempted to light up when you get there. In the great days of radio either side of the last war, celebrities were often photographed at the mike with a cigarette in hand; smoking was supposed to add to the texture of your voice. These days, most studios are strictly no-smoking, and many broadcasters find that, far from enhancing their performance, tobacco smoke makes them cough on the air. It can also set off the fire alarm.

If you have been invited to the station from which the programme is being, or will be, broadcast, you will almost certainly be in the same studio as the presenter and some, if not all, of the other contributors. This is a big advantage: you can pick up on their body language, and as the discussion unfolds you have a good idea of when it is right to interrupt. Contributors on the line from home, or in another studio, can hear only what the listeners hear, and it takes an accomplished presenter to keep them in the discussion. So if you can, head for the studio.

Once in the studio, you will be seated at a table with a mike in front of you and the studio manager, operating the machinery from behind a soundproof glass wall, will ask you for some 'level'. This is to make sure that when you start speaking, your voice will come across neither too loud nor too soft. Give them a few words: what you had for breakfast or how you got to the studio will do fine. If the level isn't right, you don't need to do anything yourself – the mike will be brought nearer to you or moved further away. You must resist the temptation to huddle nearer to the mike as you warm to your subject.

There is one thing you should double-check when you get into the studio: that you are not also being televised for the Internet. A number of radio stations have taken to installing webcams in their studios so that live pictures of interviews can be broadcast on their websites, or even on television, and they do not always alert the interviewee to this. If they do and you have no objections, you should treat the interview as if it were being televised, with particular reference to your appearance and mannerisms. But some neglect to ask interviewees' permission, so you should check. The BBC, incidentally, recently issued strict guidelines to their own stations on webcam use in radio studios: the key point is that an interviewee being filmed must be told.

As with television, you may find that the programme is already under way when you enter the studio. You will be slipping in to take the place of an interviewee whose part in the programme has finished, while the show goes on. Producers try to orchestrate such moves while the news headlines are being taken from another studio, or while a taped package, a trailer or an advertisement is being broadcast. But you should nevertheless be as quiet as possible; live radio is a seat-of-the-pants operation and the wrong button on the console gets pressed surprisingly often. During the 2001 general election campaign, a *Today* reporter pressed the wrong button in a studio in Yorkshire and was heard by the locals – who had tuned in for their breakfast programme – cursing and swearing as he tried to edit a report.

If you are in a different town or city from the presenter, you will probably broadcast from a remote studio. Not all such studios require technical expertise on your part: Broadcasting House in London has a suite of four, used mainly for broadcasts to the regions, which are controlled by a team of studio managers; in these you merely have to put on a set of headphones (or 'cans') and wait. First, the producer of the programme will come on to make sure you are there, then they will pipe the programme to you and, before you know where you are, you will be live. If nobody comes on at all from your programme, there is a number you can ring and a technician will come in to sort things out. The crucial thing here is to remain alert and ready to speak while the programme is being piped down to you and not to let your attention wander; if you get too fascinated by some item just before your part of the programme, you may miss your opening cue. And there is no worse way of being caught out on radio than not paying attention. It is harder to keep the initiative when you are in a separate studio from the presenter and the other participants, so you need to be extra alert for your chance to intervene.

Just as television can unnerve interviewees through the use of remote cameras, radio has developed the torture of the 'self-op'. This is a small studio without access to a studio manager, where you simply dial a number for central control and are then patched through to the programme you are due to appear on. Once you are through to them the procedure is exactly as with the remote; the problems arise when the 'feed' to Glasgow, or wherever, does not come on. Generally you can have this remedied by calling control once again, but on occasion the people at the other end have neglected to arrange for the 'feed', and on a couple of occasions I have left the studio without being interviewed because the connection could not be made in time. All you can do in these circumstances is keep your cool – the staff will be doing their best to put things right against the clock, because nobody likes their programme to be marred by technical hitches.

On the air

You are seated at the baize table in the studio. The mike is in front of you, a plastic cup of water is within your reach and in the centre of the table is a dull green light. When it lights up, you are live and anything you say will be broadcast. If your programme is being pre-recorded, the presenter will make sure beforehand that you are comfortable, tell you, 'We'll start on green', and when the light comes on he or she will introduce your part of the programme. If you are delivering a talk that requires no introduction, the producer will motion to you when the light comes on that it is time to begin.

From this moment, you need to *make every word count* to maximise the impact of your argument. You may have only a couple of minutes to get your case across, so you need to state it clearly and succinctly and flag up your soundbite early, in case it is the only chance you get. Having done so, you can then marshal your supporting evidence as time, and the flow of the discussion, permits. And if you get a chance, do it again.

How you speak is almost as important as what you say. If you sound interesting, your audience will be interested. You need to *speak warmly and steadily*, not too fast and certainly not too loud. It also pays not to sound shrill: Margaret Thatcher lowered her voice to prevent this happening, aware that women tend to come over on radio less well than men with their deeper timbre of voice. And while you shouldn't over-project your voice, which will make you sound grotesque, you should give extra emphasis to your most important points.

The audience can't see you, but you can establish a relationship with them even if you are being questioned by a third party. Tony Benn, a past master at the medium, habitually does this by slipping in the phrase 'what everybody listening at home wants to know is ...' as an overture to the audience. Even if they disagree with him, it works. Some interviewees always address the interviewer by their Christian name; don't unless you already know them or you are in an informal programme where 'Mr Vine' rather than 'Jeremy' would sound odd – it smacks of insincerity and doesn't play well with the audience.

There are mannerisms you need to avoid on radio. The occasional 'um' and 'er' makes you sound thoughtful and can buy you time to think in answering a question, but too many of them make you sound hesitant and unsure of your argument. There are other phrases you can use as you gather your thoughts, like 'Well, let's look at this in more detail'. A phrase like that is better, and less patronising, than 'Does that answer your question?' or 'I'm glad you asked me that', while 'I'll be perfectly frank with you' merely conveys the impression that you are being anything but.

A small minority of interviewees think so slowly that you can almost hear the wheels grinding in their brain – that's fine if it's the oldest inhabitant in the village reminiscing, but not for a politician, a business leader or a prize-winning scientist. You should also try not to lick your lips – the mike will pick up the sound; a sip of water will ease the dryness and, as long as you put your cup down quietly, it will go undetected. If you have papers in front of you, don't rustle them. And don't break wind audibly; the mike will pick up the sound to your eternal embarassment.

Without being aggressive, you need to *gain the initiative*. You should listen carefully to the questions; you can ask for a repeat if you are not clear what the interviewer is driving at, or you are quite entitled to say: 'I think what you are asking me about is X. I think this is very important, and so, I am sure, do many of your listeners. And my opinion is ....' – and then you launch into that soundbite of yours.

If the interview or discussion is being recorded, you can ask to take a question again. And if you stumble over your words, you can pause, apologise for fluffing and restart what you were saying. The producer won't mind unless time is very pressing. But be careful: if you do break off and restart, you may well find your train of thought has gone and you are less confident than before of what you meant to say. This applies particularly if whatever you just said has reduced everyone in the studio to hysterics. It happened once to me on the BBC World Service when I inadvertently spoke of the 'torpedoing of the Argentine crooner *General Belgrano*': a good five minutes went by before I and my producer, now the BBC's Head of Policy, could look each other in the eye without collapsing.

If you misspeak when on live, just plough on. The audience will forgive the odd verbal slip, as long as you don't descend into total gibberish. And you can just about get away with saying: 'Sorry. Can I start that again?' It's certainly easier to do it on radio than on television. The same goes if you have inadvertently said something unfortunate. If you have set out to describe someone as a 'shining wit' and failed – as has happened even on the BBC – it is fatal to stop and try to retrieve the situation. Just press on regardless.

With radio, the pace and flow of what you say is particularly important. Try to avoid long pauses or staccato delivery, and in particular one-word answers. Even if the presenter asks you for the briefest of responses, give them a healthy sentence or two. You are perfectly at liberty to answer a question with a straight 'Yes' or 'No', if without pausing you follow up with a supporting sentence. That gives the interviewer a chance to work out what the next question would be; if you just say 'Yes' they're caught by surprise, and there will be an awkward pause which makes terrible radio.

The words you employ in presenting your argument are very important on radio – they are the only weapons you have apart from your affability and your clarity of mind. You need to *avoid negative language whenever possible*. Words like 'difficulty', 'problem', 'unable', 'lost', 'struggle' or 'defeat' all convey the impression that you are not on top of the situation. In just the same way, talk of plant closures or redundancies, particularly if no one else has mentioned them, will rebound against you – unless of course you are attacking someone else for allowing them to take place.

Many of the ground rules for a radio interview are the same as for television. Keep to the point. Be upbeat unless the subject is exceptionally depressing. Turn negatives to positives whenever you can. If you don't want to answer the question, volunteer a positive – and related – fact instead. Answer one question at a time; if the presenter hurls several at you, answer the one that suits you best. And feel free to use humour, provided you don't come over as flippant or tasteless.

Then there are the don'ts, many of them the same as I mentioned for television and for the same reasons:

- *don't volunteer bad news;*
- *don't waffle or ramble;*
- *don't lose your cool;*
- *don't get overconfident;*
- *don't use jargon;*
- *don't confuse the listeners by raising too many points;*
- *don't guess;* and
- *don't lie.*

As the programme nears its end, the interviewer may ask for shorter replies. Remember, don't give a one-word answer but a crisp, tight sentence. And if you haven't just used that soundbite of yours, deploy it one last time for maximum impact.

At the end of the programme, the presenter will say goodbye, thank the participants and the closing music will roll. It's easy to unwind, turn to the person next to you and say: 'That wasn't too bad, was it?' or 'I made a right mess of that question about global warming.' Don't. It is quite possible that your mike is still 'live' and that your words may get a wider currency than you would wish.

'Uncle Mac' of children's radio fame never lived down the time he followed his customary 'Goodbye children, everywhere' with 'And I hope your rabbits die!' On that one occasion only, the studio manager was slow disconnecting him and the illusions of a generation of kiddies were shattered. So stay quiet until the green light goes off or the studio manager or presenter tells you that you are free to talk, or indicates in some other way that the programme is over.

If you are taking part in, say, a live magazine programme, you may well be slid out of the studio while the programme is still on the air, making your move while the news or a pre-recorded package, or maybe a piece of music, is being broadcast. In these circumstances you can say a courteous goodbye to the presenter, but keep it brief so that he or she can start concentrating on the next item. You should then leave the studio quietly, looking out for cables on the floor – less of a problem than with television, but you may still find them – and shutting the door as quietly as you can.

With a programme that is being recorded, you do not have the risk of the 'open mike' that haunts live broadcasters; only in freak circumstances could your efforts be broadcast contemporaneously. But you are open to the separate danger that you may say something into the tape recorder once you think the business of the moment is over which turns out to make exceedingly good radio – and maybe very bad news for you.

5 Staging a successful press conference

The press conference is an extremely effective vehicle for communication. It enables a person or group with something worthwhile to say to announce and explain it to the media collectively, making both the maximum impact and the best possible use of everybody's time. The press conference is of equal use in dealing with the written press, radio or television, and you don't have to be a head of state or captain of industry to stage one. But as with all other contacts with the media, there is scope for such an event to backfire on you if you go into it ill prepared, or even at all.

Preparation

At the very outset, you need to ask yourself whether staging a press conference is the most appropriate way of getting your story out. Are you calling it because there is an announcement you wish to make the biggest possible splash with, or are you under pressure to make a statement because something has gone wrong?

It is generally best not to stage a formal press conference if the news you are announcing is bad, as there is a strong risk that you will be pilloried by hostile questioners. On parade in front of the cameras, especially, men and women who have taken tough decisions often come over either as heartless and overbearing or as too weak to control the media, let alone run their own business competently. Grossly unfair no doubt, but that is the way it looks. It is also pointless, as Iain Duncan Smith dicovered to his cost, to convene a press conference to tell your party to 'unite or die'. You merely confirm the impression that it is inextricably split. You should also bear in mind that journalists arriving for a press conference where you will be on the defensive are likely to be collared outside by critics among your workforce, customers or patients before they get to hear what you have to say and will come in armed with extremely damaging questions; under such circumstances you will have lost control of events before you have said a single word.

If you are up against it, the only real justification for a press conference rather than a formal statement which does not expose you to questioning is if media interest is so widespread and so justified that you have very little choice – for example, when a report is published into serious malpractices at a hospital – and where it is right for you to answer at least some questions.

In addition, could giving the press the opportunity to question yourself and your colleagues on an issue you see as positive lead to their raising others that you would rather not be asked about? I have been to more than one press conference where what looked like a win–win situation for the organisation holding it evaporated the moment a question was thrown in from left field about an unrelated and highly embarrassing issue they must have known might be raised. Indeed, the greatest threat at any press conference comes from overconfidence on the part of those holding it; the fact that you have a positive announcement to make does not mean you can walk on water, nor does it guarantee reverence from the media, who may see this as the perfect opportunity to go for your soft underbelly. You must never appear smug or self-congratulatory, no matter how good your news.

Even if there is not a cloud in your sky, you need to ask yourself if a formal press conference is really necessary. Is the news item you have to flag up as important as you think it is? Will enough of the media turn up to make the occasion worthwhile, or could you be left with an embarrassingly low turnout? If so, you would be making better use of staff time and resources if you simply issued a press release and answered any questions from journalists individually.

You will need to be clear at the very start as to what exactly you want to say. That sounds a truism, but surprisingly, the question of what to say is often the last thing to be settled – even, on occasion, as the men and women making the announcement are taking their seats on the podium.

The golden rule with a press conference, as in any other contact with the media, is to make just one substantive announcement so that your message is not clouded by reporters seizing on subsidiary issues you consider less important. As the Labour pioneer James Maxton said of public speaking: 'Dinnae put too much meat in your pie.' Often the message is obvious, but if you are launching something complex like, say, a local authority's annual budget, you are giving out so many facts at once that you cannot expect every reporter present to adopt the same priorities. (If you are going to be sending out a number of messages of varying degrees of complexity, you may find it worth calling individual journalists beforehand, suggesting they look out for particular points of interest and inviting them to call you back after the press conference if they need any further facts not explained there.)

Preparing your own introductory statement, or a press release for distribution at the press conference, will concentrate your mind as you set down on paper the key elements of your announcement. Pitch the priorities in that statement more or less right and most of the media will follow your lead – but if you are unclear as to what your story is, don't be surprised if either you don't get much coverage or the reporters in attendance veer off at a tangent.

The thrust of your announcement, and of the press release (see

Chapter 6) accompanying it, should be the same; otherwise you will confuse your target audience. Each should contain, and concentrate on, the basic facts you wish to put across. Suppose you are going to develop a new shopping centre: you should state the precise location, the size of the site, what shops and other facilities will be included, how much it will cost, how long it will take to build, how many jobs will be created, and what benefits it will bring to the community. You should sum up all the advantages and the benefits of your scheme in a sentence or two; this will be your soundbite – the message you want the radio and television reporters, in particular, to take away with them. It should appear early on in your statement, and also in the press release as your supporting comment to the facts. Memorise it beforehand so that you do not have to look down as you say it, for this is the part of your statement that you want to appear on the next television news bulletin and you want to be able to look the cameras in the eye.

Your own statement will probably be longer than the press release and be a little more personal in tone. However, it should not be egocentric unless the announcement is about yourself, and unless you have a very complex set of events to outline it should not last more than three minutes or 450 words. The more you say at the outset, the greater the scope for obscuring your key message. You should stick to the facts and your assessment of them, and avoid any excursions into humour – jokes and comic asides always work better in the cut and thrust of media questioning, provided they are appropriate to the tone of the occasion.

You should bring the colleagues most closely involved with what you are announcing into the drafting process, turning it into a brainstorming session on precisely what ought to be said from the rostrum: how much detail to go into, and what areas of the subject those making the announcement need further briefing on. Ideally they should be armed with a little more information than they are likely to need, but should stick to the basics on the day unless asked by questioners to elaborate.

Once your statement is ready, you should get it printed out in type large enough for you to read comfortably – say 18 point. Nothing looks worse than someone burying their nose in the text as they make a major announcement.

Don't forget that a press conference is a two-way process. You have your announcement to make, but you are also inviting questions. So if there are obvious queries arising from what you have to say, make sure you have answers ready. Get someone in your organisation to play Devil's Advocate and raise all the most difficult or awkward questions a reporter might come up with, and rehearse – if you have time – how to deal with them. Remember, one question poorly answered can undermine your credibility with every other reporter present.

Having settled how the announcement should be made and explained, you need to decide who should do the announcing. Resist the temptation to do it all yourself: one person taking the rostrum alone implies to the average journalist an overweening ego or lack of managerial back-up; neither message will do your image much good. So unless the announcement purely concerns yourself, it is best to have a colleague or colleagues with you. Conversely, journalists who arrive at a press conference to be confronted by a veritable Politburo, particularly one made up entirely of middle-aged men in suits, will conclude that your organisation is riddled with bureaucracy. So never put up more people than you might actually need. On the subject of suits, remember that if the news you are announcing is bad, you and your colleagues should avoid wearing bright or cheerful colours or really outrageous ties. The rules on dress should be the same as for a television interview (see Chapter 3 above): if your clothes don't suit the cameras, your time on the air may be kept to a minimum.

The size of the platform party should reflect the extent to which what you have to say needs explaining. Three to five is a good number. A typical company announcement might involve the chief executive and the finance, sales, personnel and technical directors. If there are legal ramifications, either make sure that one of your team is fully on top of these issues or put one of your lawyers on the platform. But whomever you put up, make sure they know their stuff.

Charities and pressure groups, in particular, like to put up celebrities at press conferences to add appeal to their message. You certainly stand a better chance of getting picture coverage for your cause if, say, Joanna Lumley joins the campaigners. But celebrity endorsements are hard work to organise, and they also entail an element of risk. Many organisations that have staged a celebrity press conference (not, I should stress, with Ms Lumley) have had the occasion backfire when the celeb in question has wilted under fire from the media or made statements that undermine or contradict the cause they are supposed to be supporting. So if you are thinking of inviting a celebrity, try to ascertain as tactfully as possible whether they really share and understand your aims and how likely they are to stay on-message; if you cannot be sure of this, forget it.

The same applies to any press conference staged jointly with another organisation. It may seem a great idea for your charity or pressure group to join forces with, say, Greenpeace to make some announcement, or for you to face the press together with your commercial sponsor. But you need to make absolutely sure that, if it is your press conference, you keep control – there's nothing more galling than opening the next day's papers to find that you haven't got a mention while the group you invited to share the platform has hogged the limelight, or seized the opportunity to make a sexier announcement.

You should also make sure beforehand that everyone on the platform, even from your own organisation, is quite clear who is in charge, who will pick up on particular types of question and whether there is any relevant information that is confidential or harmful and should not be disclosed, least of all on the record to the massed media. These things established, it is worth, if you have the time, getting practice in farming out the questions, and rehearsing some of the key answers. As with a radio or television interview, you should identify the central point you wish to make, agree on a soundbite and have it ready to use.

It will probably make sense for you to chair the proceedings yourself. But it may suit you, as it generally does Prime Ministers and senior figures in business, to have your PR person or press officer sit next to you. Knowing the media, they can select the journalists who are likely to ask the most sensible questions and assure you of the most positive coverage, and act as a filter to stop daft or malicious questions getting through. They may also have a better idea than you of when to farm out questions to other members of the panel – and when to stop. At the very least, if the media present are not well known to you and your colleagues, that person can make a formal introduction, explain ground rules for the photographers, draw reporters' attention to the press release and other documentation that has been prepared and then turn the proceedings over to you.

You should bear in mind, however, that your press officer may be better occupied meeting and greeting journalists as they arrive, making sure the photographers behave themselves during the event and negotiating bids from the media for you to do interviews after-wards. In such circumstances, you would be best advised to introduce the event yourself.

You next need to select a time for staging the press conference when what you have to say stands the best chance of getting reported. Fixture clashes with major news stories cannot always be avoided; the timing of train crashes and the deaths of prominent people impossible to predict. But it is crazy to organise a press conference that clashes with, say, a major local sporting event, the State Opening of Parliament, the Budget or the aftermath of a general election. If in doubt, get someone to ring the news desk of your local paper well in advance and ask them how busy their diary looks for that day – unless making the call will trigger speculation or leaks that would torpedo your planned announcement.

The time of day when you stage a press conference will determine how much coverage you get. The best time is around 10.30 a.m., to give journalists ample time to get there, and television crews enough leeway to feed their film into the lunchtime bulletins. Failing that, early afternoon can be quite useful; you have in effect missed the evening papers, but you can expect a decent show on the teatime news bulletins and, hopefully, in the next morning's papers. If you start much later than 3.00 p.m., you will begin to miss those bulletins and fall foul of newspaper deadlines.

Where you stage your media event is also important. Unless the location is the whole point of the story – such as when Ben Nevis was reopened to tourists after the foot-and-mouth outbreak in 2001 – it is a waste of time staging it further away from newspaper offices and television and radio stations than you have to. All you will do is reduce the media turnout and leave those who do attend with deadline pressures that may prevent them doing a fully professional job. If there is an obvious picture angle – for instance, if you have concluded a sponsorship deal with your local sports club and the youngsters are out there training – it is sensible to hold the press conference on location, though you should always have space available under cover in case it rains. But it is no coincidence that most organisations hold press conferences at their headquarters or at a city- or town-centre hotel.

Next you need to make sure you get the media turnout you are looking for. If the announcement is non-controversial, the best thing to do is issue an Operational Note (see Chapter 6 below) to the media in general, and follow it up with phone calls to make sure every news organisation that might be interested is fully aware of the event and can make arrangements to send a reporter, photographer or crew. If you think the announcement would be of particular interest to specialist journalists – say, financial, political or sports correspondents – ask them individually or through their specialist desk. But even if you make contact with them all by phone, you should also fax or e-mail them details of the event – many journalists turn up at the wrong place or at the wrong time if they have nothing on paper to remind them. In issuing your invitations, you need to take a judgement on whether to reveal why you are inviting the press. Tell them too much beforehand and your event will be of little value. You will also have lost control of the story.

If your announcement is controversial, you should be careful who you invite apart from the main newspapers, the Press Association and television and radio stations. The media have a politically committed fringe, mainly freelances and journalists working for small campaigning titles, who regard press conferences – especially with companies whose activities they disapprove of – as an opportunity for grandstanding and disruption on their part. Most other journalists regard these people as a pain, but they can easily hijack your media event and deprive you of control over your own announcement. So if you are planning to announce an arms contract with some Third World dictatorship or the planting of further GM crops, confine your invitations to the established media – or think twice about staging a press conference at all.

At the venue

The time you spend at the venue setting up a press conference is crucial to the success of the event, but many organisers leave these

123

preparations to the last minute and come unstuck as a result. In particular, you need to have access to the room well in advance so that television crews can set up; let them in too late, and either you will find out that you lack some basic need of the electronic media like enough sockets, or they will still be jockeying for position when the event should be starting. You should also allow yourself enough time to set up any visual aids – and to run through them to make sure the slides in the box are what you think they are, or that your laptop is totally compatible with the projector.

First of all, though, you need to be sure the room you choose is suitable for the purpose. Clean, well but not blindingly lit, not so large that a healthy media turnout would look lost, nor so small that if even half the journalists you have invited turn up, some will have to stand at the back. You should be able to deduce from your advance contacts with the media roughly how many to expect; pick a room they – and of course your panel – would come close to filling, with a few spare seats just in case. Make sure, too – and many organisations forget this – that you leave an aisle clear so that you and your colleagues can reach the podium unimpeded and that the roving mike – if you have one – can circulate.

Most rooms are rectangular, and some have a stage at one end, theatre-style. If there is a stage, use it. But if there isn't, you should consider a less orthodox layout, with your team of spokespersons taking up position behind a table along the length of the room. It is essential for you to be able to see, identify and relate to your questioners and for them to see you, but over and over again this simple imperative is ignored through a poor layout. The Department of the Environment used to stage press conferences in a long, thin room with the Minister making the announcement at one end; television crews and photographers formed a phalanx across the room and many newspaper reporters had to sit behind them, unable to see or be seen. They got frustrated, and their reports reflected this mood. This could so easily have been avoided.

Photographers need to get their pictures without trampling on each other, so you should allow them space to spread out behind the written media, as well as allocating fixed positions for television cameras in the centre. Some photographers will want to come to the very front for close-up shots of the person making the opening statement; you should let them as long as they don't stay put and hamper the rest of the proceedings.

Before choosing your room, you also need to check for conflicting noises. Is there a choir or a ballet class rehearsing in the next room, or in the room above? Are there workmen drilling in the road outside? If there are, either get in touch with whoever is causing the noise and get them to stop it for the duration of the press conference or, if you can't take that risk, switch to a quieter room.

Once you have settled the layout of the room, you need to organise the facilities. Generally, you and your colleagues will be seated at a table, on a low rostrum if possible, and there should be a cloth on that table reaching down to the ground. That will not only hide the table legs but avoid any unfortunate shots of female colleagues who are wearing short skirts. You should have a backdrop to prevent viewers being distracted by some irrelevant detail behind like a window or a poster for another event; it can be either a plain one, or better still a logo or banner announcing who you are and the essentials of your message. But as with the background for a television interview, don't try to cram too much wording onto it, and make sure none of your panellists is sitting beneath a phrase like 'years of failure' that could undo all your good work.

On the table, it is quite in order for each of the panellists to have a small bottle of water and a glass at their place – *not* alcohol. You should aslo give them a notepad and pencil so they can marshal their thoughts before responding – and take note of anything they may want to follow up with a questioner afterwards. Otherwise the table should be kept as clear as possible; you sometimes see participants in a press conference arrive and put their briefcase on the table, and this looks terrible.

It makes sense to have a small lectern on the table in front of you; it establishes your authority, and for that reason your colleagues should not have one too. Decide beforehand whether you will feel happier, look better for the cameras and have more presence with the written press if you stand to speak. If you are on the short side and a tabletop lectern would hide you, or if more than one of you needs a lectern, you should organise a separate podium of comfortable height to one side of your table to which you walk in turn to do your presenting. For a major occasion, you may wish to use an autocue; if so, practise beforehand to make sure you don't end up racing the words on the screen before you – and when you get there, have someone make sure it works.

If there are to be visual aids, they should be projected onto a screen on the backdrop between the rostrum and the table. You need to check that the screen is big enough for your purposes, and if you have slides or other visual aids check that they are what they are supposed to be and in the right order.

If you are expecting a sizeable turnout, you may want to amplify your voices. Don't lay on mikes simply for radio: a radio reporter will either plonk a mike of their own down in front of you before the event begins, or count on a separate taped interview once you have given your general briefing. But if you have any doubt over whether your voices will carry, it is worth having mikes on the table which all your panellists can use. And if you do, for heaven's sake test them before the media arrive to make sure they work – time after time, the impact of a press conference is ruined because of amateurish setting-up of the sound system. And if you have hired an exhibition company to organise the mechanics of the press conference, never assume that they have got it right. It is far better to test everything and make the event a success than to have to bawl them out afterwards for letting the proceedings go pear-shaped.

If your organisation has an in-house sound system you have the option of getting miked up, just as you would for a television programme, so that the sound quality is better. There are advantages to this in terms of audibility – though practical difficulties for women as many dresses simply do not have anywhere to attach a mike close enough to where the words are coming from, or a pocket for the mini-transmitter. But remember – the second you are miked up, there is always the chance that somebody may pick up on your innermost thoughts.

It is also well worth getting someone reliable to tape-record the proceedings. Even if you don't expect the subject to be sensitive, you should keep a record of what is said. And if the acoustics of the room aren't brilliant and there's a crowd of journalists attending, it's also worth bringing in a roving mike so that everyone can hear the questions clearly.

The whole purpose of a press conference is to get the media on your side, so what else should you do to assist them? For a start, you should have ready a press release outlining the main points of your announcement, backed up if necessary by a pack of explanatory material, a couple of usable photographs and maybe a map or sketch of what is envisaged. You should make sure there are enough copies available for everyone who is likely to turn up – though never so many that reporters who do attend can see a forlorn heap of unwanted literature.

You should designate someone to be on hand to distribute the press releases and check if the reporters need any further material. That person can also greet journalists when they arrive, and take their names (or you can put out a book for them to sign) so that you can maintain contact afterwards. You should welcome journalists you haven't invited; even if a known journalistic troublemaker turns up, he or she will secure you more adverse publicity if you try to throw them out in full view of the rest of the media than if they manage to slip in a hostile question. Margaret Thatcher always scored points with the media for being unfailingly courteous to a very irritating man from Israeli radio.

Your greeter should also ascertain who would like a separate interview with yourself or a specialist colleague once the formal briefing is over. Television and radio reporters are particularly likely to ask for such interviews; this format enables them to look as if they have had exclusive access, and also to take the issue forward once they have heard what everyone else has had to ask. Sometimes they will keep their killer question for such an interview, rather than ask it in the presence of all their rivals. It is best if you set aside a separate room for such interviews, and you should also make sure in planning the press conference that you have left yourself time to do them. Generally, each interview will take no more than three or four minutes, but it will take television crews a little while to reposition their equipment after the press conference and get their set-up right.

Journalists who have turned out for your press conference will appreciate it if there are refreshments ready for them. You don't have to lay on a banquet: coffee, tea, water and Danish pastries or biscuits are quite sufficient, or sandwiches if you are staging the event at lunchtime. Too much refreshment for the media looks bad, particularly if the news you are announcing is grim. You should also make sure the food and drink are on a table a little away from the action to help the circulation of people and guard against spillages. And allow the hacks enough time to consume it before the proceedings start – there is nothing worse than a chief executive making an important announcement to an army of chomping, slurping reporters.

Even more than refreshment, your guests will be after information. If you have explanatory material ready for them, it makes sense to distribute it as soon as they arrive so that they can develop lines of questioning. If you leave it on their chairs, they won't look at it until they take their seats just before you make your opening statement and you will be confronted by an audience that isn't listening to what you have to say but has its nose buried in your publicity material.

You also need to think about facilities for yourself and whoever else is holding the press conference. Unless you are staging the event at your own headquarters, you need to reserve a holding room for yourselves so that you can prepare out of sight of the media you will meet. Ideally you should arrive through a separate entrance to forestall questions on the doorstep from reporters, which would puncture the impact of the event you have gone to such trouble to stage, and to avoid any confrontation with protesters. You should also get there early enough so that you have time to run through the key issues one more time before you start.

The holding room should also have access to separate toilet facilities from the media – it's as bad to be grilled by a journalist in the Gents or the Ladies as at the door – and a mirror in the room itself for last-minute checks on your hair and general appearance. You should organise coffee and biscuits in the holding room to put yourselves at ease. But you should avoid alcohol – there is nothing worse early in the day than a reporter smelling booze on your breath – and anything that is sticky or could stain: it's all too easy to arrive in a clean white shirt, but get to the rostrum with a smudge of jam on it from an overfull doughnut, or a blast of tomato ketchup from a bacon roll.

In that final run-through you should check that you have a copy of your statement in large enough type for you to read comfortably and that the pages are in the right order; there's nothing worse than realising in full flow that you've jumped a page or delivered the same one twice. Double-check any facts or local pronunciations you are not sure of, and as the media arrive ascertain from your greeter whether any of them look set to cause trouble or are flagging up questions where you can score easy runs by giving a helpful answer. If you are up to deadline and one of your colleagues hasn't arrived, get someone to cover for them and start on time unless their participation is absolutely crucial. Double-check also that there is a seat on the rostrum for everybody who will be taking part – nothing looks worse than a seat left empty or the arrival of a key player for whom a chair has to be found as the assembled media look on. It makes their participation look like an afterthought and casts doubt on your overall competence.

Before going on, you should take the opportunity to make sure you have memorised your soundbite. Read through your announcement one last time to make sure you don't trip over any awkward words or phrases; if you do, change them. Then go to the toilet, make sure you've got your reading glasses (if you need them), check your appearance one last time in the mirror, look at your colleagues to make sure they have done likewise, then put out your cigarette (if you smoke in your press conference it will be taken as a sign of nervousness), switch off your mobile or pager and ask your colleagues to do the same – and stride confidently but not arrogantly into the room.

The press conference itself

You have walked up the aisle, taken your seats at the rostrum and placed your statement on the lectern, ready to read. But before you and your colleagues say a word, there are one or two things to remember.

You will need to look and be attentive throughout the proceedings. Don't let your mind wander. Keep good eye contact with your audience. Make sure you can see a clock, but don't keep staring at it. Don't look out of the window either, but move your gaze around. Never stare at a single journalist throughout the proceedings: it will unnerve them. Your body language must exude confidence, whether the news is good or bad; it is better to lean forward interestedly than to sit up ramrod-straight, but you must take care not to slouch. If you are standing up to speak at a rostrum, you should keep a good upright posture with your feet not too close together. You should be animated but not hyperactive; the less wooden you are, the more authoritative you will seem.

Your speech should be firm, clear and well projected, particularly if you have no mike – and if you want the cameras to move in close on you when you get to a particularly important bit, drop your voice slightly.

The first thing to do is to make sure that the representatives of the media know who you and your colleagues are. Either get your press officer to make the introductions, or do it yourself. Set any ground rules at this stage: if you need to impose a time limit on questions or are ready to do individual interviews after the formal proceedings are over, this is the time to say so.

Your first words to the media should be words of welcome. You need not be too effusive, but 'Good morning' on its own is a little curt. So say how pleased you are to see them and thank them for taking the trouble to come. Now you can make your announcement, confidently and firmly. Be conversational; don't look or sound as if you are simply reading what is on the paper before you. You can smile if the news is good. If it's bad, adopt a serious demeanour;

failure to do so will make you look callous. But above all, never look bored – if you aren't interested in your own subject, why should the media be?

Next you should make your statement covering the essentials of the issue. Pace yourself – don't gabble – and emphasise the right bits; it is fatal, especially for television coverage, to look and sound as if you are reading out something you have never clapped eyes on before. This impression will be all the greater if you bury your nose in the text. So establish eye contact with your audience at the start, in mid-statement and again as you finish – just as you are repeating your soundbite.

You should then invite questions. In order to take and keep control, you should try to build a relationship, an empathy, with the journalists in front of you. So unless the event is one of total grimness, be friendly and slightly informal; if you know the reporters' names, use them. Keep that good eye contact. Be as relaxed as seems appropriate and allow yourself the odd shaft of humour – but resist the temptation to ridicule any questioner who has missed the point, unless it is clear the other reporters present regard them as a pain.

If the questioning gets tough you must, above all else, keep your cool and your temper. The moment you lose it, your demeanour rather than what you have gone there to announce risks becoming the story and you would have done better not to meet the media en masse. So be polite and firm with aggressive reporters; if they overstep the mark, the rest of the media will start taking your side.

Should time permit, as it often will, it is courteous to let every journalist who wishes to ask a question do so. If not, you should try to make sure that every major news organisation represented gets a shot – and the local paper if the story has strong local resonances and it might otherwise be outgunned. At some point in the future –

say, if you run into planning problems with the local council or some residents' group turns against you – you will need them on your side. If you have reporters present from the BBC, ITN and Sky, you should take one question from each – and try to work your soundbite into the response. Almost invariably, what you say in response to their question will go straight into their next bulletin. If they ask you a second question, it probably means they are trying to get you to say the same thing in a way that will look or sound better. You sometimes find that one reporter with a special interest in the subject or a bee in their bonnet starts to hog the questioning. If you let them, the rest of the media will lose patience first with the questioner and eventually with you, and you will lose control of the situation. In such a situation you should allow them a couple of questions, but suggest if they keep pressing that they discuss the matter with you afterwards. If they still persist, simply call a question from someone else to restore the momentum.

Your press conference may seem short to a reporter trying to get in a question, but it will seem very long to you. You need to keep your message in mind and remain in control. If you start feeling frazzled or your nerves begin to play up, take advantage of the one 'prop' on the rostrum with you – your glass of water. Take a sip as you are speaking and you will slow things down, gaining greater control.

In answering the media's questions, you should above all stick to the subject. You have set up the press conference to put across a clear message – don't cloud it with irrelevancies. You should avoid jargon, and when technical terms are unavoidable you should explain them, or ask one of your expert colleagues to. If you don't know an answer and none of your colleagues volunteers it, tell the questioner you will get back to them with it as soon as possible – and make sure you do so. Best of all, take one of your staff there and ask them to track down the answer before the press conference breaks up.

If reporters start leading you off at a tangent, steer them back to the point – using your soundbite again to remind those present why you have invited them. You are perfectly at liberty to tell a questioner if their point is irrelevant, but you shouldn't refuse outright to answer – if you do, other reporters may suspect you have something to hide and start pressing the irrelevancy further. And no matter how relaxed the atmosphere becomes, you should resist the temptation for excessive candour; more than one press conference has gone pear-shaped because someone on the rostrum has revealed some item of bad news that was not relevant or did not need to be divulged. In answering reporters' questions you should endeavour to be informative; if you seem evasive, it will tell against you in the coverage not only of that journalist but of the rest. At the same time, you should keep your replies fairly succinct and to the point – you are not there to tell them all you know, and if you ramble you will harm your image as a person and dilute the message you called the press conference to deliver. You must also resist the temptation to turn the tables and ask any of the journalists a question: the moment you give a questioner the floor, you run the risk of losing control. And above all, you should not let yourself get trapped into an argument. If a difficult questioner tries to drag you down to their level, say firmly but politely that if they would like to continue the conversation afterwards you will be happy to do so; more often than not they won't bother once they have lost their audience.

Your chemistry with your colleagues on the rostrum is also important. Your joint appearance, even if you are firmly in command, has to be and appear to be a team effort. If your colleagues are there on the platform you must involve them – nothing looks worse than the lead person hogging all the questions while their colleagues look on like dummies. You should farm out to the appropriate person any question covering their special field of responsibility – but you should be careful not to pass a question to a colleague who can't answer it. The panel should also help each other. If you see a colleague struggling, you should signal as tactfully as possible that you would like to add something. Don't interrupt, and above all don't contradict anything that a colleague says – that will give an impression of disunity and lack of control. If you need to correct anything that is said, be tactful and say you're explaining it further.

Occasionally you see one participant in a press conference quietly trying to settle old scores with a colleague he or she detests, and the message that conveys to the media (not to mention their colleagues) is disastrous. So even if you can't stand a fellow participant, remember: a press conference is not an opportunity for infighting or backstabbing, nor for letting a fellow panellist stew in their own juice in order to advance your own career prospects. And if you value your job, don't be too quick to correct the boss.

Every panellist should remember that the person in the lead is the focus of the event, and should resist the temptation to seize the media limelight. Your boss won't like it, and the media may see your bid for stardom as a distraction. So allow yourself to shine in a cameo role in support of the main speaker, but do no more than that.

Throughout the proceedings you need to stay alert. At any moment the focus may switch to you, and if you're staring at your nails or doodling on your notepad you will let the team down by looking unprepared – or worse still, not being able to pick up on the issue that has been under discussion. Supporting panellists should be just that: they should not only listen when colleagues are speaking, but look interested. If they fidget – gripping the paper in front of them is a particular weakness of press conferees – or yawn, they will be sending the media a powerful negative message about the event, the subject under discussion – not all subjects are inherently interesting – and the person doing the talking. Moreover, at any moment your special subject may come into focus, and you will need to have been listening for your answer to ring true.

You can usually sense when a press conference is running out of steam: the questions start to dry up and your audience begins to fidget. If this point is reached, you should ask for one further question and, having answered it, bring the proceedings to a close. If the questions just keep on coming and you feel the time has come to wrap things up, you should say that you know some of the media are on tight deadlines and offer to take three questions more. This puts the media on their mettle to come up with the strongest questions that haven't yet been asked, and if anyone wastes the opportunity they will attract the blame. It also gives you a chance to fit in a question from any journalist who has an obvious stake in the issue, whom you have so far overlooked. Beware of closing a press conference prematurely because you don't like the questions that are being asked, but most journalists know that if the killer question hasn't been asked in, say, twenty minutes, it is very unlikely to be.

Having given your last answer you should politely brush aside further attempts to question you. You should thank the media for coming – no matter how hard a time they have given you – say that your staff will be on hand to answer any further questions, then stop.

The very first thing you should do is make sure your microphone or sound system is off. You don't want some over-candid remark about how dreadful one of the journalists was or how one of your team fouled up on an answer to become the lunchtime headline in place of the story you called the event to promote. Then you should leave the rostrum in orderly fashion – either for your holding room, for a location outside where you and others involved can pose for further pictures, or for the point in the hall or the separate room where you will do any follow-up interviews.

In such interviews the important thing is to restate your key message. Any journalist worth their salt who has sat through the press conference and read your literature will have developed follow-on questions, and decided which of the key facts you have raised they wish to emphasise and probe: the number of jobs to be created by the shopping centre, which shops you hope to attract or some planning or environmental difficulty that could arise. You should use this follow-up interview to repeat your soundbite, particularly if the questioning turns negative or veers off at a tangent: this will be your final chance to assert control.

As with any other contact with the media, the end of the press conference isn't the end of the process. You may well find that media who couldn't get there or did not appreciate the strength of your story will ring up wanting to catch up with the story, and you should have someone nominated to assist them. You should also monitor the coverage, on radio, television and in the papers, both to assess the impact you have made and to determine whether there is any more you need to do. You may well find, having seen the coverage, either that there are points of correction or explanation you should take up with some of the media involved, or that some of the journalists who attended have a feel for the story or an interest in it and are worth cultivating in the longer term. You can then start work on a media strategy to see you through the project, right up to the far-off day when your new shopping centre opens its doors.

6 Putting out an effective press release

The press release is a fundamental tool of relations with the media. It has been around for well over a century, and while it is now delivered as often by fax or by e-mail as by hand or by post, its effectiveness remains as great as ever. For its function and purpose are to inform the media of your choice of the basic facts of the story that you wish to interest them in, or about which you are being pressed or invited to comment.

Press releases take several different forms, announcing everything from the resignation of a Prime Minister to a new packaging for a soap powder.

There is the release sent out by an organisation announcing that a new member of staff has joined, a contract has been won, a report issued or a corporate decision taken. There is the release in which you applaud the action of some other body or individual and seek to support or take credit for it. There is the reactive release in which acclamation, disapproval, informed comment or condolences are voiced following an event or decision involving others. There is also, as discussed in the previous chapter, the release put out to coincide with a press conference, setting out the main facts of an announcement for the benefit both of journalists who are present and of others who are unable, or not sufficiently interested, to attend. And then there is the straightforward public relations puff: an effort to get into the news columns or onto the air some event, factoid or product which has no news merit beyond the ingenuity with which it is marketed.

There is one further kind of press release which is purely advisory and not intended for publication: the Operational Note informing the media that an event – say, a press conference, briefing or photocall – will be held at a particular time and place on a given subject and that they are invited to attend.

Preparation

Every newspaper, radio and television station in the country is deluged daily with press releases from the highly important to the totally un-newsworthy, and you will want to make sure that yours is acted upon, not binned along with the dross. So how do you go about making sure that your press release gets noticed, and gets results?

As with any other form of contact with the media, you first need to ask yourself if it is sensible or worthwhile to go down this road. Is anyone out there really going to be interested in what you have to announce? Is announcing it simply going to fire up or irritate some group that could cause trouble for you? Is the timing right, or would you be better to wait a few weeks until there is more to announce or some difficult issue outstanding has been resolved? And, above all, what precisely do you want to announce?

Important people in business and public life often want to issue press releases to heighten their own visibility, without having anything new or specific to say. Press officers are frequently tasked with making bricks without straw, knowing perfectly well that the media can sense instantaneously if nothing is really happening. Equally, the culture of many large organisations leads to press releases being issued for the sake of it. News involves novelty and change; press releases reiterating something the media already know or which have nothing of essence to say are doomed to failure, yet still they get issued. When I first joined the *Daily Telegraph* I was called by a high-profile charity who dictated a brief press release to me. I read it back to the news editor, who responded: 'All they're saying is that they've had a meeting.' No news, no story.

You needn't have a major announcement to make. Often some quirky item of news can attract the media's attention, particularly on a slow day. So if your organisation is doing something offbeat, it's worth putting out a release. But remember: the press will instantly tell the difference between a novelty and a stunt.

As with press conferences, you don't want to try to make more than one substantive point, or you will confuse the media. It's best in a press release to stick to one subject; if two distinct issues come up at once, issue two separate press releases, if possible on different days. If you put two stories in the same release, one of them will usually die the death.

Content is not everything; your press release needs to look appealing. Too many organisations give no thought to this side of presentation and imagine that a stark, typewritten sheet of A4 with nothing to distinguish it will make their point for them. But except for very rare and grave situations when two paragraphs of large type speak for themselves – say, in announcing the death of a well-known person – the more noticeable your press release, the better. You don't, however, want to produce something so busy or confusing to look at that people start wondering what you're on; it must be both distinctive and easily readable to have maximum impact. So stay clear of fussy borders, unusual typefaces and psychedelic colours. Be simple. Be bold.

A strong letterhead, preferably in colour, gets you off to a good start. If you have a logo, use it – though not so large that you don't have room for the text. Below that you need a bold headline explaining what your story is about – and then you give the salient facts.

Critically, you want to get those facts onto the first page. Don't design the release in such a way that journalists have to turn the page before they get to the meat of the story; they may not bother. For this reason, unless it is essential to the story, don't put a photograph on the front page of the release and relegate the text to page two. If you need to issue the photo, do so separately, paper-clipping it to the handout. There is a good practical reason for this: newspapers like photos they can reproduce, and they won't be able to do this if you send out one that's printed on ordinary paper. Equally, many photos circulated with press releases are so unimaginative or poorly composed that few newspapers will use them: I repeat my strictures against the standard shot of the newly appointed executive with a telephone to his or her ear, but there are other photographic clichés that regularly turn up with press releases and merely make your company or organisation look boring.

You should give the media the facts first. If you need to put out photographs, maps, biographical details or any other explanatory material, put together an information pack in a folder – and make sure the press release is on top, even if your chief executive thinks his portrait is more important than the announcement being made.

Your release needs to get straight to the point, and stick to it. BBC trainers always instance a Home Office news release that went for two pages before disclosing that a prison governor had been fired because of lapses of security at his jail which led to two IRA men escaping. There was, as I recall, no headline at the top – just one lengthy sentence, full of subordinate clauses, about how the Home

Secretary had asked an official to investigate an incident at the prison, about which the press release was none too specific. The remit of the inquiry, the decorations held by the investigator and the name of the assessor who worked with him were all given in the fullest detail – and then, halfway down page two, came the announcement that the governor had been sacked.

If the aim was to deter any journalist from reaching the punchline, the exercise failed. Nevertheless, when reporters are busy or up against a deadline, they may not be quite as thorough as they should be and a deliberately anaesthetic press release could just achieve its objective. It is not, however, a course I would ever recommend: if you send out deliberately dull press releases, regular consumers in the media may treat on the same basis the one you really want them to read.

Most turgid releases have been put together by people who are simply not used to working with words. So think at the outset who in your team is good at expressing themselves on paper – and if nobody springs to mind, ask yourself if someone outside the organisation whom you know and trust could do the job better. A retired journalist would be ideal, and they could also advise you on whom the release could most effectively be sent to. However, you may simply have to do the job yourself, and if so, these suggestions may help. And if, when you have finished, the end product still looks boring, or if you are finding the topic impossible to explain in simple words, bin it – you may simply not have anything interesting enough to say.

Writing the release

Let's assume you want to announce that you're developing that exciting new shopping centre. Sit down with a blank piece of paper or screen in front of you, and work out what is the key point you want to make. That point will be your headline – a headline that should normally include a reference to yourself. So at the top you would write:

Stegosaurus plc to create biggest-ever shopping centre for Cambridge.

Nothing else in your story matters enough to go into the headline. Nor is there anything you could have left out: who you are, what you are doing and where you are doing it are the very essentials. If you have already made that initial announcement, your press release might concentrate on which retailers are to open there, the start of construction or completion of a particular phase of the project. Again, your headline will say no more than that.

The body text of the release needs to include all the essentials of your message, in lively but not hyperactive language and written in such a way that a really lazy journalist could cut-and-paste it into their paper. Not many will, but most reporters appreciate a press release in a style and a language that they are used to; leave them to slice across the grain of your verbiage, and they may well not bother.

The first paragraph – the 'intro' as journalists call it – is all-important. It needs to be as punchy and informative as possible to hold the attention of journalists reading it – and self-contained enough that if a paper can allocate only one paragraph to your story, its readers will still get the point. Alistair Cooke's first editor used to get young reporters to write their story in full, then cross out the first paragraph – and all too often the intro that was left (the original second paragraph) was far punchier. You could try doing the same – I have, when a really complex story has seemed impossible to start.

It is preferable to keep your intro to a single sentence – 25 words is a comfortable length. But an introductory paragraph of up to 45 words, divided into two sentences, may prove as effective a way of flagging up those basic facts. It is important that the language should flow: steer well clear of those subordinate clauses.

What the really important facts are depend on the individual story, but generally in your intro you should be telling people the following:

- *What* is being planned, decided, opposed or supported (in this case the shopping centre).
- *Why* it is important. (Here it will be its sheer size and the range of facilities it offers.)
- *Where* the shopping centre will be built or the event you are publicising held. A general location will do for the intro; you can be specific about the exact site lower down in the text.
- *Who* is developing, announcing or condemning it. You must remember to blow your own trumpet in the intro even if your logo is at the top of the paper and your name appears in the headline.
- *When* the event will take place or the project be begun/completed.
- *How big* it will be, how many customers will benefit, jobs be created, or members of the community suffer from the project being launched or opposed.
- And *how much* it will cost.

The punchiest order for setting out these facts will depend on what your press release is announcing, but almost every release will have these in the intro. In our case the intro could read something like this:

Cambridge's largest ever shopping development is to be sited on 750 acres near Addenbrooke's Hospital, Stegosaurus plc announced today. The £20 billion centre, with 300 shops, 20 restaurants, a multiplex cinema and a hotel, will create 2,500 jobs and could be open by 2005.

There you are – almost the whole story in 44 words. You haven't given all the facts, but you have given the ones that will make the greatest impact.

Generally it is best to weigh in straight after the intro with a quote from yourself explaining why it is important and setting out your positive case:

Launching the project, Stegosaurus chief executive Martin Brown said: 'This is an exciting day for Cambridge, and for the 300,000 people who come here to shop. One of Britain's most historic cities will soon have Europe's most modern shopping facilities, offering the customer style, value and unprecedented choice.'

Every word in that paragraph is chosen with care to send out a particular message. You have stamped your CEO's personality on the project, but without giving him an ego trip. Next you weighed in with a strong positive – 'exciting'. You need a word like this to build a sense of anticipation among the media and the public, but you should choose it carefully. Words like 'revolutionary' are over the top – your shopping centre isn't revolutionary unless, for example, you are banning cars from it, in which case the words 'car-free' would probably appear in your intro. Other superlatives like 'fabulous' or 'fantastic' come across as trivial and inappropriate. 'Exciting' conveys the attraction the shopping centre will have for customers who are now restricted to more conventional outlets, and the freshness of your vision – even if it isn't.

Mentioning Cambridge establishes a local link at the earliest possible stage: you want the community to claim ownership, not feel as if you have arrived from outer space and are teaching the locals to suck eggs. Your reference to the 300,000 people who shop there identifies you firmly with the market you are reaching out to, and broadens it to people outside the city; you want to attract them, not exclude them. The reference to Cambridge as a historic city isn't just cheesy – it's a way of showing that you respect the local heritage, which you will probably be accused of despoiling, and the cultural climate of the city. And by moving on quickly to the modernity of your development, you make clear that what you plan is a worthy addition to an ancient city, not a jarring threat. Finally you are telling the customer what they will get: big-name stores and styles for which they have previously had to travel to London. And while you cannot guarantee the prices that the shops you attract will offer, it is worth mentioning good value simply to avoid giving the impression that they will be so stylish that ordinary people will be priced out.

Your third paragraph can put the project in context. For instance:

> *Mr Brown was speaking at a press conference in Cambridge after signing an agreement with the City Council for Stegosaurus to develop the shopping centre in return for building a new secondary school on an adjoining site. He revealed that financing for the project was in place, and that agreement had been reached with local amenity groups on a package of environmental and transport improvements to take effect before the centre opens.*

What do you learn from this paragraph? Mr Brown has held a press conference: that shows openness. He held it in Cambridge, underlining his commitment to the city. And he has put hard cash into that commitment by agreeing, as part of the deal, to build a much-needed new school. The reference to having financing in place shows that Stegosaurus is serious and that the project will actually happen. And by striking the deal with community groups, the company has sent out reassuring messages about its commitment to minimise the impact of its project on the local environment and to make it easier for people in the area to get around. Good, strong positives that could forestall local protests about the sheer scale of the scheme and its effect on a quiet residential area.

In your fourth and subsequent paragraphs, there are further points you should make. Which big-ticket shopping chains have already agreed to take space? Who is providing the finance? Who has designed your shopping centre? How many shoppers each day will it attract, and from how wide an area? How much parking will there be? What facilities will be provided for children and the disabled? What features will make it different from other shopping centres in the region? And – critical if the scheme hasn't yet got planning permission and could get bogged down in the planning appeal process – who have you consulted about your scheme and which local groups support you? From the outset, you are looking not just for customers but for friends, if possible influential ones.

For this reason, once you have set out the facts you consider most relevant you should include, if appropriate, supporting quotes from organisations that have given their backing. Line them up in plenty of time, and check the wording back with them to make quite sure you have pitched it right. There's nothing worse than someone you have claimed as a supporter disowning your scheme the moment it is launched, but it does happen. You should, incidentally, also check that any organisation offering its support will add value to your cause: if it is unpopular in the neighbourhood for some reason, you should give it a wide berth.

In drafting your press release, you should consider what questions the media and potential critics are likely to fire at you once your intentions are out in the open, and how best you can respond to them. Obvious negatives, for instance your involvement in some controversial scheme elsewhere, should not be raised by yourself. After all, you would hardly include a prison term for fraud in your CV, and the principle is no different. But if you can put forward some positives that will anticipate and defuse likely criticism, you should do so. For instance, you don't want to flag up the fact that 200 heavy lorries are going to have to use local roads during construction. But if you've arranged to have materials delivered by rail to keep 100 of those lorries off the streets, you should say so.

For the greatest impact, you want to keep your press release tight and short – if possible not more than two pages. So it's always worth remembering that you don't have to fire all your bullets at once. Most press releases don't announce some completely new initiative or even a major decision; they report on milestones reached and progress made. This applies whether you are talking about a concrete project like the Channel Tunnel Rail Link or an ongoing scheme like the Government's New Deal for the long-term unemployed. So keep your message simple and omit unnecessary detail. If you can't cram in all the facts, don't keep jumping on the suitcase, but keep those that seem less important for another occasion when you may want to have something to announce.

You should also avoid jargon, initials and excessive technical detail unless you are dealing with the specialist media. If you want to give a large amount of technical information, produce a separate briefing paper to be included in an information pack for those journalists who will understand or appreciate it. If you need to provide detailed background information for the announcement to make sense, put it at the foot of the press release in smaller type under the heading 'Notes for Editors'.

Before pressing the 'Print' button, you should read back through the release and get a colleague to check it too. It's easy for simple errors to creep in, no matter how hard you look, or to send out messages you don't intend. Don't forget: the 'spellcheck' on your computer doesn't check facts, only spellings. And always double-check the date – it's amazing how many press releases are dated the previous year, and it makes the sender look pretty careless.

You should also make doubly sure that it is clear who is issuing your release, and that there is a contact telephone number for journalists with queries. This is particularly important for an Operational Note inviting the media to attend an event: if they can't get through to you to check something beforehand they may decide it isn't worth coming. For this reason, too, it is vital not only to give a phone number but to make quite certain that somebody will be there to answer queries once the press release has gone out.

If your news is bad

The news you need to announce will not always be positive. And if it is downright bad, you face a challenge: you are obliged to get the facts out, but you must mitigate the impact as far as possible without misleading the media.

Above all else, you should on no account try to suggest that bad news is in fact good. The media and the public see immediately through statements of this kind, and those making them become objects of contempt and derision. Yet some high-profile organisations – banks, in particular – never seem to learn: how often have you seen a notice saying something like 'In order to improve our service to the customer, this branch will no longer open on Tuesdays'? Journalists have an innate suspicion of such announcements; in the 1970s Patrick Hutber, City editor of the *Sunday Telegraph*, formulated 'Hutber's Law', which laid down that anything billed as an improvement is precisely the opposite. So don't go down this road.

The need to be honest if your news is bad doesn't mean that you should go masochistic and wallow in negatives. You need to hold your head up high. Generally speaking, the announcement of bad news is the start, rather than the end, of a process of disclosure and news management in which you have the opportunity to limit the damage to your reputation. So when you sit down to draft your press release, you should be on the lookout for anything you can plausibly say that will convince journalists that, despite what you have to announce, you are acting responsibly and with sincerity.

The classic scenario concerns the closure of a factory or a heavy round of redundancies – a decision taken for commercial reasons (one hopes of necessity) and impacting deeply not only on those losing their jobs but on their families and the wider community. In this climate, you can hardly expect to be popular. But if you handle the announcement with tact and in a concerned spirit, you may be able to gain understanding from those affected, and the public at large – provided, of course, that your actions match the claims you are making. A good journalist can spot the difference between a closure forced on a responsible firm by circumstances and some piece of breathtaking financial opportunism indulged in with no concern for the employees.

In framing your press release, you cannot immediately go onto the front foot; if your announcement will hurt, you must say so frankly at the outset. The news you are announcing is that you are closing the factory, so your headline must read something like:

Stegosaurus plc to close engineering works in Sheffield.

Don't say any more than that, and in particular don't flag up in the headline the number of jobs to be lost; you can't hope to conceal it, but you will want to discuss it in the context of your choosing, not display it as the baldest of negatives. So neither will it appear in your intro, which will read something like:

Stegosaurus plc announce with regret that their Hillside precision engineering works at Darnall, Sheffield, will close in November.

Again, the facts of the matter that you need to state: who you are, which of your plants is affected and the fact that you regret the course of action you are having to take – managements don't always. And finally the date of closure, the fact in the story, after news of the closure itself, that will matter most to your employees.

In the second paragraph you will have to mention how many people are losing their jobs, and if there is anything you can say in mitigation this is where you say it:

The plant employs sixty people. Twenty will be offered transfers to the company's more modern works at Rotherham, and Stegosaurus is negotiating with the unions a retraining package, financed by the company, for every other worker who wants it.

So now the figure is out in the open. But by the end of the paragraph the reader knows you're not throwing sixty people out on the street. One-third will stay on in apparently better working conditions, and the way you have announced the transfer to nearby Rotherham implies a continued commitment on your part to the area. By offering to train all those who are left, you are showing that you won't just walk away – this is an initiative to which you can be proud to put your company's name. And the fact that you are talking to the unions highlights the impression of Stegosaurus as a responsible employer.

Next you need to explain why the plant is closing:

> *Stegosaurus chief executive Martin Brown blamed the closure on falling export orders caused by the high pound. 'Our workforce have done everything they could to raise productivity, but it has got to the point where continuing losses at Darnall were threatening jobs at other plants.'*

How does Mr Brown come across? He has a simple explanation for the closure, and one that journalists familiar with the climate in his line of business will readily appreciate. He pays tribute to the workforce, which shows his human side and may help them as they look for other jobs. And he reveals that jobs elsewhere in the group might have gone had this particular plant stayed open; once again, an eminently fair and sensible point. There's no effort to make bad news look good, but you start feeling that Stegosaurus value their workforce and have been reacting to adversity with concern and prudence. This might not have rung so true had Mr Brown been less measured in voicing his regret. It may look sincere on a television or radio interview for you to say you are 'gutted' by the decision you have had to take or that it has been 'the worst day of my life', but don't put sentiments like that into a press release: they look glib and insincere.

In your fourth paragraph you probably need to say a little about what the factory has been producing and how long it has been doing so, with an acknowledgement to the role the plant and its workforce have played in the local community. It may also be relevant to detail the size, total workforce and remaining plants of the Stegosaurus group; that puts the closure into context. You may want to reassure your customers and the rest of your workforce by stressing that, despite the closure, the outlook for your company as a whole remains good. But if you have been showing a healthy profit, do not include the figures in the press release – or people will start asking why you couldn't afford to keep the factory open.

What else should you say about the closure that will both inform the media and the community and demonstrate that you have done and are doing all you can to lighten the blow? You may decide to say no more for the time being and make subsequent, entirely positive, announcements about, for instance, any success with other local employers in finding jobs for the workers you can't relocate or any initiative in concert with the local authority to redevelop the site in a way that will boost the local economy and employment. Many employers who have pulled out of an area have nevertheless left behind a fund of goodwill because of the sheer decency they have shown in honouring their commitments – and provided you are actually doing this you can make sure, through your dealings with the media, that you take appropriate credit.

There is just one more point of paramount importance. If you are announcing bad news to the media, you must make sure that, by the time the press, television and radio get to hear about it, the individuals concerned have already been notified. If your workers hear of the closure first on their local radio station, they will feel they have been treated with contempt and will convey this view forcibly to the media – wiping out any presentational advantage you might have gained through a skilfully worded press release.

Sending it out

You don't simply draft a press release and fire it off into the ether. You need to decide carefully when it should be sent out and to whom it should be circulated.

Sometimes you have no control over the timing. An event has happened – say, a leak of poisonous gas at your factory – and it is essential for you to comment on it. In that case, speed is of the essence; the sooner you can get out your version of the facts, the less the opportunity for anybody else to get to the media before you and cause trouble. But you must match speed with accuracy, making sure not only that your statement is correct and appropriately pitched but that in your haste you do not offer up any hostages to fortune. And don't forget: get someone else to check what you have written before it goes out.

If your press release is announcing a coming event, you need to issue it well enough in advance that you don't miss the deadlines of any of the media that are likely to be interested. For a community event, this means at least a week beforehand to make sure that your local weekly doesn't miss the opportunity to publicise it. Similarly, for an Operational Note advising the media of your event so that they can send a reporter or photographer rather than because you want advance publicity, you need to allow enough time for news and picture desks to plan it into their diary – 48 hours is reasonable.

If your announcement is not time-sensitive, you need to work out when the media would be most likely to carry it – a Monday morning, for example, or a quiet day in the holiday season. If your story is market-sensitive, you will probably need to release it when the Stock Exchange is closed, which generally means in the early evening. You should also make sure that the news reaches the media at a time when you, or one of your staff, are ready and available to speak to them.

It is important that all the media, as far as is practicable, are able to run the story at the same time; if some of them use it first, the others may not bother. This doesn't mean that the release has to hit every news desk simultaneously; that would be impossible to arrange. What you can do is insert a line in heavy type at the very top, above your headline, saying:

> *This news release is embargoed until 3.00 a.m. on Friday 17 August.*

What this means is that any news organisation to which you send your release is asked not to run the story prior to that time. Setting the embargo at some time between midnight and 6.00 a.m. may seem pointless, but it is the fairest way of putting out a story you are instigating. Its practical effect is that morning papers are free to carry the story, with copy based on your press release having been prepared the previous evening, and that radio and television can start covering it in their breakfast bulletins. If the story is a big one and you do not wish word of it to leak out in the hours before publication or third parties to be approached who might seize the initiative from you, you should add a further phrase, that:

> *The media are requested not to approach anyone about its contents until after that time.*

Wording like this appears on the highly sensitive news releases on the New Year and Queen's Birthday Honours issued a couple of days in advance by 10 Downing Street on behalf of Buckingham Palace, but it is also a sensible precaution for anyone who wants to retain control of their announcement and the facts in it.

Most news organisations are meticulous about honouring embargoes. Mistakes do occur, but any paper or radio station breaching them regularly doesn't just earn the resentment of its competitors – people with facts they need stop giving them out in advance. That hurts, for with many complex or important stories the media cannot do their job properly if given the facts at the last minute, hard though they will try. So you can generally trust them to keep an embargo – though not quite so often to honour your request not to approach third parties about your announcement prior to publication. For anything really big, it is therefore wise not to give them too much notice; 6.00 p.m. for the next morning's papers or breakfast radio is fine. If you are leaving it that late, however, it is worth contacting any journalist you may particularly want to cover your story and make sure they will be available – without of course telling them precisely what it is about.

Next, who do you send it to? Which news organisations are likely to be interested? Is this essentially a local, a national or a specialist story? Has any paper been running a campaign on the issue? Are there particular reporters you should approach, or should you simply send it to the news, features or business desk? Are there non-news organisations you should send it to out of courtesy because they may be interested or may get calls from the media on the subject? Is there anyone in the media to whom you do not want it distributed, for example a journalist who has written mischievous stories about you in the past?

How should you make sure the journalists you hope will take an interest get to see your press release? To start with, it is up to you to make the approach and supply the information; after all, you want the publicity. Some chief executives expect journalists to make a personal visit to their office to collect press releases, and news desks rightly draw the line at this – they are not there to fuel your ego.

Having decided which organisations and journalists you want to target, send the release out to them by fax or e-mail, with a hard copy posted to them first-class as backup if there is time. Allow a decent interval to elapse, then ring to make sure they have got it; a surprising number of faxes never come out of the machine, and some people in key positions in journalism never read their e-mail. Your follow-up call will not only confirm to you that the news organisation has received the information; it also gives them the chance to clarify any points they are uncertain of, and you the opportunity to establish a rapport that could prove useful in future. If the organisation claims not to have received the release, resend it; double-check their e-mail address and, in the case of a fax, check with them which of their machines it will come through on. If it has arrived and they haven't read it, you have the chance briefly to commend it to them and engage their interest. But if they are quite obviously not interested, don't argue with them – if you push too hard they may serve up a negative story that does you no favours.

Just one further suggestion. It is well worth keeping a file of all the press releases you have issued. There is nothing more embarrassing than having to scrabble round to find out what you have already announced, or to discover when you have just put out a release that your predecessor at work or in the chair of your pressure group issued an identical press statement six months ago – or worse still, told them precisely the opposite.

In dealing with the media, consistency is all-important.

7   Now it's up to you

There is more to dealing with the media than being interviewed by newspapers, radio and television, staging a press conference or issuing a press release, but these are the interfaces you are most likely to experience, and the techniques I have outlined will between them serve you in any contact you have. For they are, as I said at the outset, based essentially on common sense.

By the same criterion, these same techniques have a wider application beyond the confines of dealing with the media. You will find that press conference techniques come in handy if you are called upon to chair a public meeting – doubly so if the media turn out to be present. Others among these tips will come in handy if you are making a speech to a gathering where the cameras are present, for example, or giving a presentation to colleagues or clients. In these situations you should take extra care that the pages of your speech are in the right order and that you have switched your mobile phone off. One Zambian Minister whom I media-trained was in full flight before the cameras when his mobile went off; he did his best to redeem the situation by answering it as briefly as possible and then cracking a joke about it, but by the time his audience had stopped laughing they had completely lost the thread of his argument.

In all your dealings with the media your essential need is to be in control, to get across the points you want to, to disarm your critics and to persuade a wider audience of the merits of your case and of your sincerity. I hope you will find in practice that these techniques work for you, and that as they do, your confidence in handling the media will grow. As that confidence grows, you will in consequence communicate your message ever more effectively – and that will be of help not just to you but to the media you are dealing with.

Journalists as a breed appreciate dealing with people and organisations who take the trouble to refine their message and put it across with clarity, and who can answer questions informatively and with confidence. After all, they spend much of their working time dealing with woolly minds at surprisingly high levels of society, business and politics. If you can establish yourself as a skilful communicator, whether at local level or on the world stage, your image and reputation with the media – and with the general public who, through them, you are trying to reach – will improve, whatever the merits of your case.

You are now equipped to deal with the media – so get out there and try it, and good luck!

Index

Acronyms 92
advertising 51–2
'ambushing' 87–8
announcements 117–8 (*see also* pres
   conferences, press releases, statements)
appearance, your 26, 80, 81, 86, 119
Archer, Jeffrey 5
Autocue (*see* teleprompter)

bad news, release of 149–54
BBC 68–69, 73, 75
   Broadcasting House 108
Beaton, Cecil 39
Benn, Tony 27, 110
Bias 20, 45–6
Blair, Tony 76
Body language 89, 131, 135
Bosanquet, Reggie 78
breaking a story
briefing 5
Broadcasting Standards Commissionl
   43
'buy-ups' 61

Callaghan, James 30
Caxton, William 48
'chequebook journalism' 59–62

Clifford, Max 11, 12, 60, 63
cold calling 5, 12
columnists 20
complaining 37–38
Conservative Party 34
contacts 17
controlling the story 9, 11, 23, 28
Cooke, Alistair 97
copy-takers 40
Corbett, Gerald 26
corrections 38–41
credibility 28

Daily Mail 50
Daily Sport 60
Daily Star 60
Daily Telegraph 39, 40
Day, Robin 93
Deadlines 48
Deedes, Lord 105
Diana, Princess of Wales 49
Diary of a Nobody 41
'doorstepping' 16, 25, 63
Downing, Stephen 45

Embargoes 156
Eriksson, Sven-Goran 103
European Parliament 36

Evening Standard 46
Excalibur 32

'facing the music' 5
'fluffing' 111–2
freelancers 10

'going to ground' (*see* lying low)
GQ 65
'grid' 8
'grow legs' 31

Hague, William 54–5, 64–5
Harry, Prince 62
Hattersley, Roy 72
Have I Got News For You? 72
Hello! 60, 64
'human interest' 14
humour 91, 103
Hutber, Patrick 150

Interviews (*see also* questions, panel
    discussions)
    'ambush' 87
    at home 83–4
    at work 84
    challenging the interviewer 27 (*see
        also* Paxman, Jeremy)
    in the studio 80–81
    on air 88–9
    on location 84–6
    use of language 26
    what to wear 26 (*see also* televi-
        sion)
ISDN 104
ITN 68

Jaffa, Max 39
Jargon 92, 148
Journalists (*see*:reporters)

'killing off' 39
'kite-flying' 35

Labour Party 30
Lawton, Tommy 39
leaks 35–37
Legge-Bourke, Tiggy 62
libel 41–2, 101–2
lies 94
lip-reading 86
lying low 4, 24
local news 9, 11
local newspapers 1, 2
local radio 1, 2
local television 1
losing your temper 93

magazines 14
make-up 80
Matlock Mercury 45
Maxton, James 117
McKenzie, Kelvin 2
'media scrum' 22
media training 51
meeting reporters 21–3
Merton, Paul 72
Ministry of Defence 36
Mirror 54

national press 9
negative language 112
negative puestions 91

News of The World 60
news stories (*see also* press releases,
    press conferences)
    breaking 5
    fresh 2
    human interest 6
    local 2, 5, 6
    novelty 6, 140
    targeted 2, 9
    timing 2, 5, 9
    topical 6
news agencies 10
news organisations (*see also* newspa-
    pers, magazines, television, radio)
    approaching 12–13
    locating 13
Newspapers
    bias 45–6
    deadlines 48
    features 14
    local 1
    space allocation 48
"no comment" 3, 25, 92
non-news media 64–66
Nott, John 93

'off the record' conversations 20
OK! 60, 62
Operational note 122, 139

Parkinson, Cecil 4
Paxman, Jeremy 27, 70 (*see* chal-
    lenging the interviewer)
Phoenix the calf 69
phone-ins (*see* radio)
photocall 9

photographers 52–6, 125
'pool' of reporters 22
PR Disasters 23–24
    British rail and the lost dogs
        49–50
    Dickens, Geoffrey MP 12
    Sheffield bus services 24
PR handlers 11 (*see also* Clifford, Max)
Press Complaints Commission (PCC)
    20, 43, 62
press conference 8, 115–37
    answering questions 132–4
    backdrop 125
    catering 128
    chairing 121
    closing 136
    effectiveness 115–6
    holding room 129
    introductory statement 117–20,
        131–2
    layout 124–5
    location 122, 124
    overconfidence 116
    platform party 119–121, 135
    preparation 115–23
    press pack 127
    role of press officer 121
    roving mike 124
    technical requirements 126–7
    timing 121–2
    use of celebrities 120
    who to invite 123
press release 8, 127, 138–57
    deliberately dull 142
    distribution 154–7
    embargoes 156

explanatory material 141
headline 143
importance 138, 139
'intro' 143
proofreading 149
releasing bad news 149–54
technical information 148
timing 154–5
types 138–9
using photos 141
Privacy 62–4
and public interest 62
public relations firms (PR) 10 (*see also*
PR disasters)
Pyke, Magnus 89

Radio 97–114
comparison with television 97
discussion programmes 106
'don'ts' 113
effectiveness 97–8
establishing an audience relationship 110
fluffing 111–2
intimacy 97–8
jokes 103
mannerisms 111
microphone technique 107, 110
mistakes 112
notes 104
phone-ins 98–102
preparing for interview 102–9 (*see
also* interviews)
'self-op' 109
speaking 110
webcam 108

winding-up 113
Radio Authority, the
radio car 103
rebuttal 29–35
remote studios 81–2
reporters
assaulting 24
dealing with 15–16, 20
freelance 10
getting rid of 17
keeping in touch with 8
local 10, 18–19
meeting 20–21
objectionable or rude 20
qualities of 18–20
selecting who to talk to 12
talking to 6–7, 14–16, 20
types of 17–18
Ridley, Nicholas 58, 91
roving mike 124

Saga 64
Scott Inquiry 34
Scottish Parliament 49
'self-op' 109
Shropshire Star 38
'soundbites' 74, 76, 90
specialist publications 9 (*see also* non-
news media)
speeches (*see* public speaking, statements)
Spectator 58
spokesperson 7–8
Spurgeon, Dr 30
statements 118, 131–2 (*see also* press
conferences, soundbites)

statistics 92
Sun 46, 49, 60, 62
Sunday People 62
Sunday Telegraph 36, 150
Sunday Times 51
swearing 94

taking control 23
teleprompter 82–3
telephone interviewing 14–16, 56–9
Television 67–96 (*see also* interviews,
   panel discussions)
   ambush' interviews 87–8
   autocue 82–3
   body language 89
   conducting oneself on air 88–94
   in the studio 77–83

live broadcasts 71–2
on location 83–8
payment 74
preparing your appearance 74–6, 80
regional news 68–70
studio audiences 72–3
using humour 91
winding up 94–5
Thatcher, Margaret 22, 110, 128
Thorneycroft, Lord 94
'trailing' stories 36
Twain, Mark 41
'walking shots' 86–7
webcams 108
what to wear 26, 81, 86, 119
whistleblowing' (*see* leaks)
William, Prince 62